BROKEN

A Story of Abuse, Survival and Hope

ANNE PETERSON

© 2013 by Anne Peterson. All rights reserved.

No part of this book may be reproduced or transmitted in any form or by any means, electronic or mechanical, including photocopying, recording, or by any information storage and retrieval system, without written permission from the author, except for the inclusion of brief quotations in a review.

Disclaimer: The author is not a doctor, therapist, or any other type of health professional. If you are in need of counseling, please seek the assistance of a qualified professional. This book is not meant to be medical advice in any way. The author shares her experiences as a means of encouraging others and offering hope.

Cover design by Anne and Jessica Peterson

Cover photo by Jessica Peterson
www.jessicapetersonart.com

ISBN-13: 978-1497538979
ISBN-10: 1497538971

CONTENTS

	Acknowledgment	5
	Foreword	6
	Introduction	9
1.	No More Talking	11
2.	Looking Back	17
3.	Another Goodbye	25
4.	A Bittersweet Reunion	33
5.	Appearances are Deceiving	55
6.	The Journey Continues	73
7.	Make the Pain Stop	81
8.	The Way we Think	97
9.	What does Healthy look like?	119
10.	To the Hurting	131
11.	Other Stories	159
12.	Conclusion	173
	A Letter to my Readers	183
	About the Author	185

I Want to Thank:

My friend, Bonnie for believing in me and never stepping back.

Dr. Jim Phillips for his valuable input, and for believing I had something to say.

My nephew Drew for praying and for encouraging me.

My brother George for being in my corner and believing in me.

My daughter, Jessica, for her artistic talent and her ability to edit. She is a flower to me, that will never lose its fragrance.

My husband, Mike, who was willing to let our story be told so that others might be encouraged to hope..

Foreword

In Broken, Anne Peterson captivates the reader with her incredibly insightful and fast-moving stories of life-changing events that transformed her family. The book moves so quickly that I found myself not able to take a break for fear that I would miss the lesson or the experience conveyed to us by Anne in her unique style of writing. Everyone can relate and express pain and healing. Anne provides us with insightful poems that equip us with the confidence to start a healing journey through life's challenges.

Anne covers a wide array of situations, including one that speaks to the domestic violence suffered by her sister. Unfortunately, her sister experienced the worst of these situations, and her passing caused an unspeakable grief for her boys and her family members. As a former prosecutor, and creator of the Domestic Violence Division for the Cook County State's Attorney's Office, I believe that there cannot be enough written to console the families of intimate-partner-violence victims. To be abused by the individual whom you trusted and selected as your life partner is a crime that transcends all crimes.

"Negative people drain us. They are like withdrawals from the bank. We need positive people who'll make deposits in our lives." This is one of many powerful messages from Broken. I read those lines over and over again. All of us have toxic individuals in the circle of our life that we interact with on a fairly regular basis. Taking a step back to evaluate whether those individuals are making deposits or withdrawals in our lives can be life- altering. It is a brilliant way of organizing and evaluating the people in our lives.

Whether you are a victim of domestic abuse or have a loved one that has experienced abuse, this book will elevate you to a place where you can learn and start to heal. Anne's focus in this book doesn't end with abuse victims. She touches upon intimate details with her husband, her parents, and herself. It is a broad scope of candidly and selflessly sharing an array of issues that affect all of us. We all have pain and suffering at various points in our lives. This book is sure to touch and stay with its reader. Although I have spent over twenty years studying domestic violence issues, after I finished
Anne Peterson's book, I turned it over and started again. Anne gives many lessons and shared experiences regarding the struggles of healing from a variety of abuses. Not one word can be missed or forgotten.

Pamela Paziotopoulos, former Supervisor, Domestic Violence Division, Cook County State's Attorney's Office (Chicago)

Introduction

Some books simmer quietly in the corner of your mind till it's time to pour the finished product before your audience. Some books need to be coaxed onto the paper.

Gingerly, the words tiptoe on blank pages. And there are still other books that beg to be written, with an urgency unable to be silenced. Sentences jump with abandon. This is one of those books.

Life is hard, isn't it? Some things I thought would happen didn't; other things I never imagined materialized before my wide-open eyes.

Life doesn't end with brokenness; that's where it begins. This book is from my sister and me. She's not here anymore, but it's from us, just the same.

I want to share my story with you. It's a difficult story, but one I need to tell. It's about being broken.

Maybe you're broken too. The good news is, we can grow even when we're broken. We're not finished. Life is a process.

It's difficult to put years of your life between the pages of a book. You'll find I do a lot of flashbacks. It's only to give you a better understanding of how things were.

1. No more Talking

Peeking out from cream-colored drapes, I watch the mailman. On days he doesn't stop, I hate him.

Running to our curbside mailbox, I pull the metal lid down. Yes. A letter from my sister, Peggy. I wonder what she'll tell me about her boys today.

Her letter seems light—short and to the point. Bad news often is.

"This is going to shock you, but I'm getting a divorce."

Well, she's right. I *am* shocked. I have to talk to her. Pressing the numbers I know by heart, I hate the miles between us. I loved it when we were both in Illinois, and we talked to each other every day. I hate the army for bringing us here to Colorado.

I barely say hello before she blurts out, "I can't talk now, he's harassing me again!"

In the background, I hear her husband, Bob, taunting her. What's going on? I want to scream. Instead, I hang up, saying, "I'll pray."

She's already left the conversation—left before it started.

Those two thousand miles feel like a million. My stomach resembles a six-year old's shoe laces. I pace, but it doesn't help.

I run to my friend Cindy's house two doors down. Once inside, I blubber my news. Anxiety makes me feel that wherever I am, it's the wrong place. After just a few moments, I tell her,

"I need to go home, "If Peggy calls, I need to be there."

Retelling the story doesn't help. But at least I'm doing something. I have to do *something*.

Is she alright? Should I call again?

The day just drags on. The ten o'clock news comes on T.V., and my phone rings.

"Calling the police was easy," Peggy says. "I wish I would have done it sooner."

I can finally breathe. She talks for ten minutes before she says, "I need to go." Something about running up her bill. That's my sister.

I hang up and redial. "Okay, now it's *my* dime. Talk."

She bleeds one story after another—stories I'm hearing for the first time. I cover up my mouthpiece so she doesn't hear me crying.

"Anne, he waits till the boys are asleep, and then starts in on me."

She hardly comes up for air. How did she keep this to herself? Why?

"Anne, once we were at a lake. I came out of the water and he said, 'How *was* it?' I told him, 'Really nice.' And he said, 'That's not what I'm talking about, I saw the way you were looking at the lifeguard.' I said, 'Please Bob, the family is here.'"

Peggy tells me of her stifled plans to become a realtor. Her tennis outfit cut in shreds. Suspicion and accusations.

She almost whispers, "Anne, one time, while the kids were asleep, he held a knife to my throat."

The hairs on my arm stand on end. The knot in my stomach tightens. I can hardly breathe.

Without pausing, she continues, "Anne, I *have* to tell you what else he did."

There's more? I'm not sure I can take any more. And she's the one living it.

Peggy continued, "We had an agreement whoever was watching the kids could stay in the house. The other would stay with a friend. I was at Shelley's house when Bob called me and said, 'You're not planning on coming home right now, *are you*?'

The house was quiet when I walked in. On the counter I saw a pie in plate I had never seen before. In our bedroom, he had another woman. I got so angry I started screaming. I picked up the pie plate to throw it at him and he said, 'Don't *wreck* that, she *made* it for me.'"

I let Peggy talk till her words ran out.

She told me our brother Gus came over; he had a wooden axe handle in his hand. Then the police came, and Bob left.

I was exhausted. She had told me her tragic marriage in one hour. My insides hurt.

"I'll talk to you later," I told her. "I love you."

"I love you too," she said.

My emotions are all over the place. I'm sad, overwhelmed and relieved—all at the same time.

God, please help my sister.

Until that call, I had no clue what she had been going through. My stomach churns as I undress. Will I even fall asleep? Little did I know, once I hung up that phone there would be…

No More Talking

*"Divorce" the letter read
"Violence"...it went on.*

*A long-distance call made:
"I can't talk now! He's harassing me again."
Hours later a phone rings and two sisters talk.
One tells of a hurting heart and ten years of pain,
The other sobs in silence.*

*"Calling the police was easy,
 I wish I would have done it sooner."*

*Days later another call. "She's gone.
 No one knows where.
 She never showed up at work.
 Her husband says she just walked out."
Disbelief fills a sister's heart.
Too many questions invade her mind:
Why would she leave her kids?
Why didn't she take her car?
Why not wait for the money
that would be hers the next day?*

*Some questions in life get answered,
and some take time.
It has been thirty-six years
since two sisters talked,
And one still hurts.*

2. Looking Back

I'm five and Peggy is three. We tuck our cotton dresses into our underpants, pulling out only the edges. In our eyes we are sleek, beautiful ballerinas.

"Keep your legs stiff," our dad says.

One at a time, he lifts us high in the air. Our arms outstretched, we own the world. For now, everything seems okay. Seems.

A Ballerina

I wish things were different
—that I stayed a little girl
who stood on your hand like a ballerina.
But you changed all that,
and I won't dance for you anymore.

Things change: stressors, never-ending bills, a struggling business. Whatever the reason, life becomes hard, sometimes painfully hard.

It always starts the same. An air of apprehension permeates the room. We run in different directions when we hear the yelling. Terror fills our eyes—terror mixed with confusion.

And then there's shame. As children, we carry shame as well as we're taught. Guilt is another jacket we slip on.

Peggy and I lack a softness. We want to feel safe. We're learning the art of self-protection. We hear the screams of whoever's being hit—the pleading,

"Dad, please stop!"

"Put your hands down or I'll give you something to *really* cry about," he yells.

No wonder we're afraid of sudden movement, hating surprises. Noise is a warning sign. When noise increases, our adrenalin pumps. Hide and seek starts.

Dad is a large man—to us, huge. His powerful hands have learned how to hit, and he has mastered it. He grabs his belt off the hook, or yanks it out of its loops.

We tried to hide his belt, but it didn't help. He used his hands instead. Hands which forgot how to lift ballerinas.

Peggy and I feel dad-less. He's not there for us. That's okay; we'll look somewhere else.

Everything changed

I'm sixteen, tired from my shift at the snack shop with Dad. All I want to do is go to bed. I'm not even going to church tomorrow, I decide.

Is it 8:00 yet? Is that clock broken?

Finally, I bag the freshly made hamburgers for hungry mouths at home. I walk the few blocks home in the cool November night.

Walking in, the food is grabbed from my hands.

"Is your father okay?" my mom calls from their bedroom.

"Yeah, but he was crabby."

I lay on the couch, uniform and all. Just wanting sleep. But sometimes, we don't get what we want.

My brother Gus yells out to me, "Mom's calling you."

"No, she's not," I respond. It's a game we often play, but I'm not in the mood for any games tonight.

Gus retreats to his room downstairs, and I fall asleep. A couple hours later my dad's large hands shake me.

"Where's your mother?" he demands.

"She's in your bedroom." I answer with agitation.

Once more I try to get to sleep. But once again he's at my side.

"She's not there," he announces, "where is she?"

"Then she's in the bathroom," I yell.

Our house is not that big. Why does he keep bothering me?

In the morning, instead of waking up to Mom's cooking, I wake up to a conversation.

"Dad, you've got to *do* something," Gus, my eighteen-year-old brother pleads. "Something's *wrong* with her."

"She'll be okay," my dad mutters.

But she wasn't okay. I was right, she had been in the bathroom. But what I didn't know was that my dad found her fully clothed, lying in a dry bathtub with her arms folded across her chest, and her glasses on her head.

When my dad found her there, he put her in bed, where she belonged. Even when she fell out of bed, he somehow got her back into bed. And when she wet the bed, he still told himself she was going to be okay.

But wishing doesn't change things.

Asleep

Waiting with quiet patience,
praying for some response.
Why don't you wake up?
Blurs of white uniforms,
unaware and detached,

An insensitive sun shines apathetically.
They wheel in a machine to breathe for you.
Flashing lights have people running.
Words meant to reassure do not.

Silent silence.
The machine wheeled out, I'm so sorry.
Tightened muscles, senseless sobbing,
Why didn't you just wake up?

Three days later we stand before an open casket surrounded by a strong fragrance. Mom used to tell us,

"Don't get me flowers when I'm gone."

Unappreciated flowers sit everywhere.

As we stood saying goodbye to the one person who held our family together, I thought I could never feel worse than I did at that moment. But I was wrong.

About a month later, Gus was having lunch with my dad and me and he started talking.

"Dad, remember the night mom got sick?"

My dad looked up.

"Did you know she called Anne and Anne didn't go?"

My dad's eyes turned to steel. He looked over and pointed at me saying,

"It's *your* fault your mother's dead."

And I took that guilt and carried it with me for years.

Even when mom was alive, our home lacked warmth. Except for scattered moments, like this one.

Mom and me

*The lights flicker on our
black and white television set.
Mom and I watch an old movie,
letting the ice cream sundaes
she brought from the snack shop
cool us on this hot summer night.
Lifting the clear, plastic lid,
I smile at the chopped nuts
squished down in the whipped cream.
No cherry, just like I asked.
It doesn't get better than this.*

Looking for love

While I retreat inside myself not dealing with Mom's death, Peggy keeps searching for her identity. She hangs around the park with Gus's friends almost every day. She likes one guy, Tom. He seems to like Peggy too. Her whole world starts revolving around Tom. She decides he's the one for her.

But Tom's not on the same page. He tells Gus on a phone call,

"Look, I just want you to know I'm breaking up with your sister."

Peggy's fragile world starts crumbling. She buys a large bottle of aspirin and goes off by herself, tired of hurting.

Gus finds her, carries her to his car, and rushes her to the hospital. They take out all traces of aspirin. Too bad they didn't take her pain.

Peggy is a broken person looking for someone to fix her. She's gets lonely waiting for the white horse to show up, carrying her prince. Where is he, anyway?

Isn't that what we both wanted? The story we heard from the time we were little?

Peggy starts considering another one of Gus' friends. She loses no time transferring all her hopes to Bob. Maybe he can fulfill her dreams. So what if she thought the same thing about Tom. He's gone now, Bob stands before her starry eyes.

And Bob is available—except not really. For Bob was left at the altar. And it becomes clear that Peggy and Bob do have something in common: both of them are broken.

Tying the Knot

At only eighteen, Peggy stands before a judge with Bob. In moments, they are married. She does not walk down an aisle with dad.

There is no big reception. Just a small gathering to start the life she thought she always wanted.

And now that she is back on course, she could move towards one of her all-time goals: children. Peggy wants to be a mom. Both of us wanted that.

Our Dolls

Peggy and I are little girls who sleep with our dolls. I cringe as my plastic child digs her fingers into my side. But, I will not put her under my bed like Peggy does I'm determined to be a better mom than Peggy.

I smile smugly.

3. Another Goodbye

It's 1976, two weeks before my wedding. The phone rings. "Anne, you've got to come and see Dad. He's dying of cancer," Peggy says.

"I caaan't," I stammer. But inside, I realize I have to.

The hallway at Veteran's Hospital in Chicago, doesn't end. My legs are like Jell-O.

What will I say after all this time?

Seven years ago is when he hurled at me his accusation. I push that scene down inside of me as I walk into his room. The hospital room is sterile, unfeeling. Like dad.

The years were not kind to him. He looks older than fifty-two, with white hair. His smile shows the teeth he has and places where others used to be.

"Annie, you came! But why do you look so mad?"

breathe in deeply. "It was *not* my fault Mom died."

"I know," he whispers, looking downward.

Countless hours, years, were wasted by the power I had given his thoughtless words.

He utters, "I'm sorry I wasn't a good father." It's the first apology he's ever said. Pictures of him chasing us with raging eyes start fading. And in their place grows an unbelievable urge to show him kindness.

I try to see life through his tired eyes. He must have been scared to death, being left alone with five children at only 44 years of age. The more I try to understand, the more pliable my heart becomes.

I don't want revenge. Maybe I went in there thinking that's what I wanted, but that was then. I am standing in now. I surprise us both when I say,

"You did the best you could."

Leaning over, I gently kiss my dad's stubbly cheek. We're reconciled. Our last conversation together—our best.

Looking Back

The more I worked through difficult memories, the more my good ones float to the surface, no longer captive.

I'm five and, Peggy is three. We live on Jackson Boulevard, where we make mud pies in our small, grassless yard. Sometimes Peggy gets so involved in playing, she forgets everything, like bathroom breaks. When she sits on the ground and gets up, there are round, dark spots on the back of her shorts. I form an anti-Peggy club and she tells Mom.

"You don't do things against your sister. Never do things against your sister," Mom scolds.

Our kitchen set

It's Christmas. We just opened the best gift in the whole world—a kitchen set made of white, corrugated cardboard: a fridge, a stove, a sink, and a cabinet, all for us.

Normally, we opened our gifts around midnight on Christmas Eve, but not this year. Mom and Dad didn't finish putting together our kitchen till three o'clock in the morning, even with Uncle Steve's help.

The sink's faucet has a sprayer like that on a Windex bottle. The plastic burner on the stove glows orange when you put a battery in. Mom saved empty food containers for us. This was the best Christmas ever.

You can have George

"Let's play house. I'll be married to Mark (our cousin) and you can be married to George," I announce.

"I don't *want* to be married to George," Peggy pouts.

But I didn't want to be married to George either.

"But Peggy, you can even kiss him 'cause he's our brother."

"Ewww! I don't want to kiss George!" she whines.

No one does, Peggy.

Rice Street

We've just moved to Rice Street. Grandpa and Grandma don't live here with us, but we have room to run. We even have a swing set. Early in the morning, Peggy and I go out to swing, singing at the tops of our voices. That memory warms me, like the sun warmed our faces.

I wish that I was young once more,
that I could find that childhood door;
I'd swing so high above the trees
and never would come down.

There are many kids in our neighborhood. We have fun, no matter what we do.

The Circus

*Our neighbors started coming
tickets in their hands,*

*There wasn't any music;
there was no marching band.*

*Our circus was a little one
consisting of just three;
my brother George,
who was the clown,
my sister Peg, and me.*

*Our audience was rather small
—I think there were just eight,
but we were so excited
that we could hardly wait.
I was the trapeze artist,
without the greatest ease.
And up on top our swing set bar,
I hung there by my knees!
Our audience was new to this
as far as we could tell,
so we would tell them when to clap,
and tell them when to yell.*

*And when our show was over,
those thirty minutes flew.
We had a special mission*

that we all had to do.
We took the money we had earned
—a dollar eighty-nine—
and went into the bakery,
and proudly stood in line.

For there beside the register
was sitting all the time,
a small container with the words:

Please Give to March of Dimes

With other people watching us,
we dropped our money in.
It was the biggest thing we did,
we couldn't help but grin.

Of all the games we ever played,
and all the toys around,
we never had such fun as when
the circus came to town.

The Sculptor

I'm twelve and watching my siblings again. I'm too old to play with dolls, too young to stay up late. Old enough to babysit, too young to be paid.

Okay, fine. I'll watch George, but I'm not playing with him. He's being a pest.

So I come up with a plan.

First, I enlist Peggy, who is ten. We grab a dictionary, looking for the perfect word. It has to be a word George doesn't know and one that sounds like a bad word.

We agree on the word "sculptor," especially when we see the naked statue next to the word. We wait for George to tease us. It's not a long wait.

"You make me so mad! Do you know what you are? You're a . . . a sculptor!" I yell.

I gasp, "I'm sorry! I didn't mean it, please don't tell Mom!"

A smirk spreads over his face. Stomping away, he gloats, "Wait till mom gets home, are you gonna' get it!"

Success is sweet

Time crawls when you're waiting for something special. Peggy and I play a board game till mom comes.

Before she puts her packages down, George is in her face.

"Mom, do you know what Anne did?" He waits.

"She called me a *sculptor*!"

With no expression mom says, "So?"

Peggy and I fall to the floor laughing.

My brother became a husband, a father and a teacher. But to me, he'll *always* be a sculptor.

Peaches

Mom is remodeling the basement. She's papering one wall and painting another one green.

When our cat, Peaches, saunters in, mom yells, "You better watch that cat! She can't be down here with all this paint."

Peggy puts Peaches on a leash, thinking the problem is solved. Out of nowhere, Peaches jumps in the open basement window, while still on the leash. Hanging there, she squirms against the newly painted wall.

"Get her *out of here!* m*om yells.

After Peggy lifts Peaches out of the window by the leash, we hear a gut-wrenching scream—half human, half animal. Peggy doesn't know turpentine burns when put on a cat. Peggy starts bawling.

"I don't know how you'll *ever* be a mom, if you can't even handle this," mom says.

4. A Bittersweet Reunion

Our brother, Steve, is getting married. It's a hot, sweltering day with just family and friends attending. We're all nervous. We're about to see Peggy's boys for the first time since she disappeared. Steve made it happen.

Bobby, one of Peggy's sons, is now a teenager. He approaches us and leans in saying,

"Has anyone seen our mom?" He tries reading our faces. We all stand there for a moment and I finally respond,

"Bobby, we don't believe she's *alive,*"

We can tell he's surprised. It was then we realize we were not all on the same page. They were told their mother left them. We knew that wasn't true.

Our reunion is bittersweet. We're glad to be with the boys, but it reminds us of how much we miss our sister. Now we re-establish our relationship which was severed. And we answer any and all questions we can about their mother. It is so good to reconnect. We know she would have wanted it this way.

One day a friend of mine called me. She had been on a train when she met someone from church who was a Private Investigator.

"My friend's sister disappeared years ago," she tells him.

And TJ tells her, "I'd love to know more about that."

So all of us get together and talk about getting my sister's missing persons case re-opened as a possible homicide.

Puzzle pieces

I sit with the police report from 1982, trying to fit all the pieces together. I'm not good with puzzles.

Here is another report; here is the conversation I had with her. They have to go together somehow.

But how can they? I'm missing pieces. Without them, I'll never see the whole picture.

Pouring over the pages, I weep. No one should have to read about their family in a police report. No one.

A Wedding

It's 2004. I'm holding a wedding invitation.

"Mike, my sister's son, Bobby, is getting married in Minnesota. I really want to go."

Mike tells me, "I'll take you. But don't expect me to talk to his father, Bob."

"That's fine," I tell him. "Just get me there."

Sitting in the church, I notice a photograph of my sister placed on the altar. It's a picture I had never seen before. Tears roll down my face. I'm angry she's not here to see her son get married.

At the reception, I approach my sister's husband. We're trying to make it seem like nothing is about to happen.

"You did a good job with the boys," I manage to say.

I'm told I hugged him. I don't remember. I walk away and finally I breathe again.

Plans can Change

I'm at Judson University, to register for classes. Completing my B.A. has been one of my goals for a while. All that remained was picking up my books from the table before me.

But instead of picking them up, I heard myself ask one of the woman there,

"When is the last day I can drop out without being penalized?"

The woman says, "I'm sorry, I don't understand what you're asking me."

I start shaking. And tears start falling.

Someone points out where the washroom is. Another person runs to get a counselor.

"Hi Anne, I'm Doris Haugen. Would you like to come with me and maybe talk for a little while?"

Sitting in her office, I notice a couple of plants and photographs on her desk. Before me is a box of tissues. She must know me.

Doris waits, wearing the warmest smile. My words get lost between my sobs. And I begin to share my story—the story of my sister.

Doris listens as my pain spills all over the place. I'm spent as I share for over an hour and a half. I tell her all about my sister's disappearance, our endless waiting, and what is in the near future.

Quietly she remarks, "I'm not sure this is the best time for you to start classes. Would you agree?"

I do agree. Forging ahead with my educational plans was not wise. My emotions were clearly driving my train. I decide it's best to wait. And part of me is relieved.

Instead of Mike picking up a returning college student, he takes home a broken, tired woman.

We keep close contact with our family members: phone calls, emails, anything as long as we touch base.

And then we get the call: Peggy's husband, Bob, is arrested. Here we go. Hearing the music from Channel 5 News makes my stomach turn. My sister's face is on television. Watching hurts. The upcoming trial is getting closer.

Support

"It would be good if you could find a grief group," I was told. So here I am in the group. Each person is very nice. We go around the circle sharing. And while everyone is friendly, I feel distance when I mention my sister was murdered.

It's true; many of us have lost a loved one. But, I feel different from everyone else. I don't fit in here. And then I hear about another group

Homicide Support Group

Walking into the Kane County Courthouse, a police officer instructs me to put my purse on the conveyor belt.

My keys are placed on the counter.

I gather up my things as the officer shows me where our meetings will be held. It will be a room I become familiar with in a short amount of time. A room I feel safe to be who I am—a family member of a homicide victim.

This monthly support group is a lifesaver for me. Attending are a psychiatrist, an attorney, and a victim advocate. The psychiatrist, Tim Brown is there to help us process our feelings.

The attorney, who alternates each month, is there to answer questions about upcoming trials or sentencing.

The victim advocate, Judy, is there for support, even attending court proceedings when requested. The members are people who have lost a loved one to homicide. We are part of a club none of us asked to join.

I smell the coffee as I approach the group each time. They are some of the most wonderful people I've ever met. People like me, whose lives were interrupted by tragedy. People desperately trying to resume their lives, hoping to move on.

"Don't put too much stock in the trial," we're cautioned. "There are multiple cases where the guilty party never went to jail."

Dr. Brown gently shares, "I have visited prisoners who never confessed their crimes. They will take them to their graves."

I see people who come in raw, scared. Little by little, they feel safe enough to open their hearts and share their stories. To heal. This is a place where we are free to express any of our feelings. No one will give us pat answers here. No one will judge.

No one cries alone here. This is my home for a few years. I feel less lonely. We're here to help each other.

I've met mothers who have lost their children, a young couple whose unborn child was killed by a drunk driver, and two sisters whose brother was killed by a gang. I've met families of loved ones who died as a result of mistaken identity.

I often cry on my forty-minute ride home. Sometimes I scream, letting my pain escape.

Thank you God for this place.

Status Hearings

My brother Gus and I sit in another status hearing. As uneventful as these meetings are, I think back to the one or two I missed.
"Don't worry Anne, nothing happened," my brother Gus tried comforting me.

But I could not be comforted. Going to these hearings is the only thing I can do for my sister. To miss one feels like I'm letting her down.

Here we go

The court date is set. We're advised to refrain from speaking to newspapers/reporters, with the exception of one: Dick Johnson from NBC news. He did the first newscast back in 1982, entering her home just a couple of days after Peggy was reported missing.

The tape shows the boys with their dad. It's a movie about my sister, without my sister. I cry watching it.

In the video, her husband, Bob, says she walked out, and he told her, "Good riddance."

No matter how many times we hear his story, we don't believe it. There's no way she would leave her boys. None.

And now, twenty years later, I'm sitting with Dick Johnson, answering questions he's chosen for me. He's a nice man. And with all my energy, I try to focus on what he's asking.

The Pictures

I watched the policeman drive away. He came to pick up photos. Not just any photos, but the ones my sister had sent to me through the mail.

I smile, thinking of what a bad photographer Peggy was. Her pictures were sometimes blurred. She'd almost cut off one of her kid's heads. It feels good to smile thinking about my sister.

The police officer just drove away with the only thing I had from her, except for a couple of greeting cards tucked away.

"I'll be careful with them," he promised. I wipe away tears, asking God to keep my pictures safe.

The day is here

Cameras point toward us as we walk into the courthouse at 26th and California. This feels surreal.

Just put one foot in front of the other. Keep going.

Will today be my turn? Or will I sit with other family members waiting in a special room. We look at my nephew Bobby's new baby— Peggy's first grandchild, Holly Jo. I hold her, feeling familiar anger rise up in me.

Peggy should be holding her. She is missing so much.

My turn

An officer leads me to a room where I am to wait alone. I start praying quietly and then I begin softly singing hymns I know by heart—hymns I haven't sung in years. Peace I cannot explain envelopes me.

Although my body is sitting in this room, alone, I picture myself sitting in God's throne room, on his lap, singing to him. I just want to stay here.

But it's time. And now, God goes with me into the courtroom. I am not alone. God calms my shakiness as I hold the photographs.

And when I point to my sister's husband, the part I dreaded the most, God helps me, just as I asked.

It's decided my testimony is done. I take my place in the courtroom next to my brother. I exhale.

We listen to testimony after testimony. One person testifies,

"There was a Canfield truck parked in front of the family home the week Peggy was missing."

While Canfield is the company where Peggy's husband worked, he did not drive a truck. He drove a company car.

Peggy's eldest son, Drew, who was nine when she disappeared, testifies next.

"In the last couple of days before my mom was gone, I'd hear my parents fighting. I once slipped out of bed and crawled on the floor to where I could look downstairs and see them. One time he held a knife in his hands. I was so scared."

Bobby, who was seven when his mom died, gives his testimony. You can hear a pin drop as he shares,

"I heard my mom scream and I ran into the house. My dad was straddling my mom, punching her in the face. There was blood everywhere.

I didn't know what to do, so I ran downstairs to the family room and tried putting my head in my arm. I just wanted to get that picture out of my head.

Within minutes, my dad came downstairs. He was crying as he washed blood off his hands. Then he told me, 'Get your brothers; I'm taking you on a bike ride.'

Later, when we came back to the house, dad told us, 'Don't bother your mother, she's sleeping.'"

"Did you ever see her again?" the attorney asked.

"No," Bobby replied.

Drew also shared that the time they were told to let their mother sleep was the first time she didn't come in to kiss them goodnight.

Day after day, we listen to audio tapes recorded by the police. Tapes when the boys met with their dad, prior to the arrest. They had hoped for a confession they never got.

Before they were wired, their dad told them,

"Just give me some time and I'll make everything right." But he changed his mind.

In the courtroom, a police officer wheels a television set up front, facing us. I tense up. Leaning over I tell George,

"I can't do this."

There on the screen, I see my sister's house. I expect her to walk out her front door. My tears start again. My brother's hand rests on my shoulder. My stomach hurts.

We hear one testimony after another. Foolishly, I used to think, if I just knew more about what happened, I would feel better. I was wrong. The more information I learn, the worse I feel.

There is a recess. What a strange word. This is not a break and it's certainly not fun. While the attorneys thought it would be a few days before the verdict would be reached, they are mistaken. Within a day or so, the judge is ready. *But are we?*

The verdict

In the quiet courtroom, I wonder if anyone can hear my heart pounding.

Judge Porter states he believes Peggy Dianovsky is dead at the hand of a crime.

But he dismisses our strongest testimonies from Peggy's sons. He says,

"If the things they shared were true, I believe that information would have been disclosed when the boys were questioned by the Schaumburg Police."

There is a sinking feeling in my stomach.

The judge throws out the testimony of one of Bob's friends, Paul, who shared that Bob asked him to get a gun, and why he wanted it.

The judge explains, "I believe if this testimony was true it would have surfaced long before now."

We are literally sitting at the mercy of this judge. Has the world stopped?

Finally he continues, "Therefore I find the defendant, Bob Dianovsky…"

Will it really be over in just a moment? All our years of not knowing? Our years without Peggy, and this last year of conversations, phone calls, emails laden with grief and sadness?

It's like a morgue in here. And trust me, I know how quiet a morgue is.

"Therefore, I find the defendant…not guilty."

The other side of the courtroom erupts in cheers. Bob's family members smile, giving each other high fives, patting him on the back.

We watch, frozen. Cameras flash pictures for upcoming broadcasts. Police officers show up at our sides to escort us to the States Attorney's office.

I walk, but don't remember moving. Is it really over? No one speaks. There's nothing more to be said.

We cry looking at each other. Now what? Are we expected to do something?

When we leave, we hug each other, not wanting to let go. My brother Gus loses it in George's arms.

Like zombies, we make our way downstairs, certain most of the reporters will be gone. Peggy's youngest son, Jon, offers to give a statement to the media.

We leave, taking all our memories with us.

At last, Peggy has been declared dead. Something we knew for years. Now it will be public knowledge.

For weeks, prior to the trial, the media hovered over us, hoping for a story, a comment, something. But once the verdict was announced, they swarmed to the other side.

In seconds, we became invisible. Just like Peggy.

Saying goodbye

It's time. We're about to do the last thing on our list.

We're having a memorial for Peggy. The gravestone was delivered, the church was secured. All we have left is to go and do it. I don't want to.

A sharp pain in my right side screams for my attention. Great! Is this appendicitis? Now?

My daughter-in-law, Heather sits on the edge of my bed, calling her mom, a nurse. No, it's not my appendix. My body is fighting the day.

I can't do this. How can I put all this behind me? It has defined me for years. If I subtract it from my life, will I even be here?

Lying down for a few moments helped, but it's time to go. I lie down in the van for the twenty-five minute ride. I have to be okay. I'm going to do something we never had a chance to do. I'm going to say goodbye to Peggy.

The chairs are set up in the lobby at Christ Community Church. It would be depressing to hold the service in the sanctuary. The number of people would be lost with all the empty seats. And we felt empty enough.

I feel sad at the small turnout. But it's been twenty-three years. It's time to share about Peggy. And so we take our turns.

Gus shares

"Peggy always looked on the bright side of things, which used to tick me off. For example, if bologna, bread, and chips was all that was left in the house, what was Peggy's response? 'Let's go outside and have a picnic.'

She also had a characteristic I really admired. She was willing to scrimp and save, doing without for a special reason, be it the house, car, or even a fancy dinner, like lobster. And once the goal was reached, she savored her reward.

Every one of her children is like her in that way. They live in the moment, plan for the future, and enjoy every minute in between. Peggy enjoyed her life and she wasn't afraid to let everyone know what a great time she was having."

I share

"I still remember when Peggy and I used to lip sync the songs, *I Will Follow Him,* and *Johnny Angel.*

We spent hours doing that and laughing in between.

Peggy was a person who could accomplish anything she set her mind on, no matter the obstacles. I admired that about her.

I remember our many conversations. She was always sharing something her boys had done. They were the joy of her life. You could hear it in every word. And she never said a negative thing about them. Never.

A really special memory was when I came over to her house. She would sit down to play the piano, when out of nowhere, her boys appeared and started dancing all over the place. The faster the tempo, the crazier they danced until they finally collapsed on the floor, laughing. It was great."

George shares

"One memory I have of Peggy is when she and I stood up for our cousin Goldie's wedding. We were six and eight years old. Peggy looked like an angel and I felt like a little bartender in my tux and vest. We were like a princess and a prince.

I also remember one day so many years later, in early summer, when I asked Peggy to give me a ride to my old school. She drove all the way from the northwest side of Chicago, to Rogers Park and back, in her yellow Volkswagen Beetle. She was expecting Drew at the time and she looked beautiful, and as always, exuded her Peggy confidence. I think this was the first time that we actually talked to each other like adults—equals.

She was so excited and looked forward to having her first child.

We talked about what was to come, and for the moment, all the promise life had to offer. We smiled and laughed a lot that day. She drove that little four speed like she was an Indy driver, and if she was in that race, she would have raced to win."

Steve shares

"I remember when Peggy used to take me trick-or-treating. One time in particular stands out in my mind.

Peggy made a pumpkin costume for me, and there I was with a green hat, green tights and a green shirt. It wasn't enough that I was already overweight, but then she stuffed the costume with balled-up newspaper. That was a good memory."

When the sharing is over, Heather slides onto the piano bench to play a song Peggy knew on the piano, *Fur Elise.* Tears fall freely.

Then my son, Nathan sings, *Give me Jesus.* It is touching and heartbreaking at the same time. He didn't get to know her.

After the memorial, it's time to go to the cemetery.
To stand on Peggy's empty grave. Bob knows where her body is, but he won't tell. The police believe she was dumped at the company's site.

George carefully places a silk flower blanket that he made over her grave. We look at the picture of her as a flower girl.

The words beg to be sung, and I give in.

When we all get to heaven
what a day of rejoicing that will be,
When we all see Jesus,
we'll sing and shout the victory.

We're leaving the cemetery now. I feel spent, like she just died. I ache.

You cannot love someone deeply and simply erase them from your life when they die. It doesn't work like that.

I used to feel like Rip Van Winkle, who awakened after a long sleep to find the world had moved on without him.

Grief is difficult. People who have lost loved ones move through their broken lives, trying to make sense of it all. Our grief was complicated. It went on for years.

It was especially difficult since we lived in Germany when my family was going through Peggy's disappearance. Letters and phone calls became so important. Gus had felt so helpless. He even contacted a famous psychic, hoping to get some answers to our many questions.

Greta, the Psychic, was known for helping the police with cases. Gus told me over the phone that Greta described in detail where Peggy's body was. Greta said "Your sister's body will surface in the spring. Her limbs will be visible."

The Unexplainable

About a week later, we were getting ready for a church potluck. I had placed two freshly baked pies on a cookie tray, atop a radiator in the front hall.

Slipping into my coat, I headed for the door. As I walked into the room, I found both pies face down on the floor. There was no reason they would fall off from where I had placed them.

Picking them up, I heard a voice say,

"*She found a pie on her counter in a plate that wasn't hers. It was an apple pie, wasn't it?*"

I felt chills and cleaned up the mess, ignoring the voice.

Once I got outside, I stepped on a branch and it cracked. Just then I heard the same voice say,

"Her limbs will be visible in the spring."

I tried to resume my day, pushing that voice out of my mind, but the eeriness refused to leave.

Once we were home, I made the long-distance call to my brother, Gus.

"I can't believe you called me right now," Gus said.

I told him about voices I heard, about the pies, and the strange feeling I had that I couldn't shake.

Gus listened quietly and said,

"I just got back from looking for Peggy's body with Gretta. I can't believe you called now."

I made a decision right then. I could talk to my brother, but I could no longer ask him about what the psychic had said. For while he was looking into things like that, I was feeling warfare on the other side of the world.

Gus made trips to the police department whenever a body was found. He was always so involved and burdened with it. He missed her so much.

With all our sadness, we still had some better memories tucked away. Sometimes it was nice to take them out and remember. Especially when they were sweet ones.

Little Mouse

My brother Gus and I giggle in bed as we pull the covers over our heads. We're six and four, playing a game.

"Pawn DEE key," we chant. (The Greek word for "little mouse").

Running footsteps get closer. Peggy flies into the room, landing on Gus and me.

She seems heavier than a two-year old. We laugh so hard we're crying. And Peggy runs out of the room to do it again.

I love when we play like this. If only we could stay little.

5. Appearances are Deceiving

"Smile. You're such a beautiful family," the photographer told us.

We sit posing for a picture for our new church directory, adjusting our plastic smiles.

I hate that picture tucked away in my bottom drawer. Appearances can be so deceiving.

That photographer had no idea what we had gone through just last week. None at all.

Sitting in a psychiatrist's office, Mike was asked, "Have you ever thought about taking your life?"

Mike was quiet. Why was he taking so long to answer this? How long could it take to just say, "No?"

Finally, Mike responded, "Sometimes I do."
What? Was he serious? This was new information.

As we left the doctor's office, I tried processing Mike's response to the psychiatrist's question.

Why did Mike say something like that?

Crossing a line

Mike, wasn't doing well. On days like this, I would step lightly, careful not to break any of the eggshells beneath my feet.

It didn't matter. Our conversation quickly went to a bad place. In a matter of minutes, his mind misconstrued things I said. In the midst of it, somehow he convinced himself I had betrayed him.

I saw his eyes change. I was looking into my father's face. A face I hadn't seen in a long time. And then, I felt a sting on my cheek. I was stunned.

I screamed, and within seconds, my son came upstairs. I told him, "Dad just…"

Nathan told me, "Mom, go for your walk."

Before I knew it, I was on the other side of the door. I walked around the neighborhood fast, hoping I didn't see anyone I knew. Mike had never raised his hand to me. Never. I didn't know how to process this.

I got back to our house and Nathan told me to get in the car. Jessica was already in the back seat. He drove us to my friend, JoHannah's house, which was just minutes away. Once there, Nathan began to shake, even when JoHannah placed a blanket around his shoulders.

Looking down, I noticed he hadn't even stopped to put his shoes on. I felt sick.

After a while, Nathan left to go to work. What he didn't expect was that I would return home.

But I knew Mike didn't mean to cross that line. I knew he would feel bad. I just didn't know *how* bad. Outwardly, I tried moving on. Inwardly, I was scared. This was new territory.

Mike's self-hatred surfaced. He was tired of all the pain he had caused us. Tired of all the yelling and screaming he had done. Tired of the anger which controlled him. But more than anything, he couldn't forgive himself for raising his hand to me. The guilt became too much.

Mike started convincing himself we would be better off without him. That everyone would be better off. Of course, I didn't know that he was thinking this it at the time.

It's Labor day and Jessica and I make our way home from the pool. Mike had joined us yesterday, but today was a different day. Today he opted to stay at home.

"I just want to be alone," he had said. "Is that okay?"

And it was fine with me. After all, we had a nice time together yesterday. He seemed to have a good time.

Jessica showed him what she had learned with swimming and he took in every moment.

"Watch me, Dad!"

And Mike responded, "That's great, Jessie." Everything the kids did was great.

I was okay with him missing it today. Yesterday was a stellar day. Or so I thought.

And now Jessica and I were done. It was a good last day. I'm glad we have this pool in our subdivision. In minutes, we were home.

I walk to my room to change clothes and notice a handwritten note taped to the door:

Please don't wake me up

Carefully, I remove the note. I hate it when tape is put on these doors. I felt proud of myself for giving Mike the time he asked for.

Pushing the door open, my eyes adjust to the dark room. But Mike's not in bed, but instead, crawling on all fours.

"What are you doing?" I ask.

Trying to get up, he crashes into the blinds.

"What's the matter with you?" I ask, as my mind tries to understand. His words are slurred.

My eyes spot the open pill bottle on the dresser.

"Mike, did you take *pills*?" I yell, tightening up.

A week ago, he had taken extra medication. I knew he was not doing well emotionally, yet I dismissed it at the time. But wanting things to be okay isn't enough.

I watch Mike fall back onto the bed.

I scream, "Nathan!" and our nineteen-year old son bounds up the stairs.

"Call 9-1-1! Dad took pills."

In moments, Jessie comes upstairs, stopping when she sees a policeman holding Mike's pill bottle. Nathan ushers her back downstairs, bribing her to clean his room.

I wait for the ambulance.

They arrive as neighbors congregate outside. One neighbor, Tim, walks in asking,
"Is there anything I can do to help?"

"Pray," I manage to say.

The paramedics push a gurney through the front door, shooting questions at me:

"Has your husband been depressed lately?"

"What kind of pills were they?"

"Do you know how many he took?"

Handing them his bottle, I watch Mike being strapped to the gurney.

"Would you like to ride with me to the hospital?"

"No!" I answer quickly.

I'll get there, but I will *not* follow an ambulance. I followed one with my mom in it. Once was enough.

"I'll take Jessie to our house," my friend Kym said, touching my shoulder.

The five minute ride to the hospital is a blur. Arriving there, I see the eight women from my prayer group at church. They've come to wait with me. My jaw aches.

Someone reaches in their purse for Advil. My stomach churns. Our pastor comes as the doctor walks toward me.

"Your husband's levels are dangerous," the doctor explains. "We're watching him closely. If they rise any more we'll have to transport him by helicopter to Chicago, We're on the phone right now with poison control."

I'm in a zone that doesn't seem real. Images bombard my mind.

I'm already picturing him gone. Because I've lost so many loved ones, death seems more real to me than life. My mom, my dad and Peggy. Death is no stranger to me.

I picture us living without Mike. I picture the struggles our kids will face because of his decision. My anger rises and holds hands with my worry.

Has it been hours I've been waiting? It *feels* like hours. Eventually the doctor reappears.

"He's stabilized…He's going to be okay," he says. "We'll be transferring him to his own room."

He'll be okay, but I wondered, would I?

They take me to Mike and the Pastor offers to accompany me. I see the Pastor talking to Mike, but I'm in a different zone. I'm still processing the whole thing.

The Pastor says his goodbyes and I stand there before Mike. A myriad of emotions swim in my head. Anger being the strongest.

"We're about to move him now. If you like, you can just follow us."

"NO!" I say too quickly. "I need to get back home."

On the way out of there I'm glad that my friends had already left. I try to hold back tears that want out, but I'm not very successful.

Walking into my empty house I let the tears fall. Crying out to God, I ask him to help me. I knew what was ahead, and I didn't feel I had the strength to take that journey.

And yet, I move forward. The journey would be long, sometimes difficult, but I knew we didn't take it alone. take alone. God would be there every step of the way. Just like he always was.

Counseling

Going to counseling is not new for Mike and me.

And while I'm thankful he's willing to get help, there's still a part of me that just doesn't want to go through it again. I remember the first time we were in that setting.

The year was 1976, and Mike and I attended a little chapel in Germany where he was stationed. They were offering a marriage workshop and we decided it would be good for us to attend.

There were six couples, including the Chaplain and his wife.

"When two people get married," he explained, "it's not just the two of them in the house. Each person brings the personalities he/she has been influenced by. There is a lot of baggage.

Baggage? Mike and I have extra pieces. We are two broken people who married. And without even knowing it, we hurt each other over and over again.

But one thing was certain. I loved Mike. And from the first time I met him, I noticed how sensitive he was.

*   *   *

It was 1971, and I was having back problems and needed to go to the company doctor. Though I didn't know Mike well, I did see him from time to time at the Bible study I attended.

"Hello Anne, This is Mike Peterson. I was wondering if you would like company as you go downtown to the doctors?"

I didn't drive at the time so it meant public transportation. I didn't mind having some company.

"Sure," I responded.

"I think the bus ride is too hard on your back," Mike said after my appointment. So he flagged down a taxi.

Mike was a musician, excellent on the guitar. Once, after our Bible study, he called me over with his guitar on his lap.

"Anne, remember the song you sang at church that time? Could you sing a few lines to me?"

And as I did he played along. He had figured out the chords to the song I created. That touched my heart.

Yes, Mike had a soft side. I saw this once when I watched his interaction with a kitten.

And while it was true that Mike had a lot of baggage, so did I. In marriage, the masks come off. Our life was a roller coaster ride. We'd do okay for a period of time. But after a while, like an unreliable car, we'd need an overhaul. Like this time.

Something is wrong

It's 1990, on a Saturday night at a church function. Social settings are hard for Mike. He doesn't feel comfortable in crowds, so I'm never sure how it will go. But church was sponsoring a family fair at the local YMCA and it will be fun for the kids.

After walking around with Jessica, who is four, we rejoin Mike and Nathan.

Nathan is trying to get a can of pop out of the vending machine and it's not cooperating. When the can got stuck, he gave the machine a slight kick. Mike thought Nathan was being destructive so he yelled,

"What are you *doing*?"

Just then, the Pastor's wife approached them asking, "Is something wrong, Nathan?"

"I'll tell you what's *wrong*," Mike responds. "I have a sixteen-year-old kid living in a ten-year-old's body. *That's* what's wrong."

My eyes widen as I watch Mike. This seems to come out of nowhere. Is this the same guy who wrestles with Nathan on the floor, till both of them collapse laughing?

This Mike seems very different. I want the other one back. I stand there surprised.

Is he really going to vent his anger here? Around these people we know and care about?

I rush to get the kids ready to go home. Embarrassment is a good motivator. I'll be seeing my counselor in a few days, I remind myself. Just hang on.

Abusive means what?

In the counselor's office I relay the story of Saturday night. She listens and then hands me a piece of paper saying,

"I'd like you to look at this sheet.

On it are listed various kinds of abuse.

Physical Abuse

Beating	Biting	Choking
Grabbing	Hitting	Kicking
Pinching	Pulling Hair	Punching
Pushing	Restraining	Scratching
Shaking	Shoving	Slapping
Excessive tickling	Twisting arms	Spanking
Using weapons	Smothering	Tripping

Power

Denial of basic rights
Legal means of forcing power
Deprivation of private or personal life

Mandated duties

Controlling the amount of bath water used

Stalking

Spying
Following to activities Extreme distrust and jealousy

Emotional Abuse

Put downs
Name calling

Mind games
Mental coercion
Extreme controlling behaviors Conditional affection
Loss of identity

Threats

Threats to end relationship
Makes threats to harm emotionally or physically
Threatens life
Threatens to take the children
Threatens to commit suicide
Threatens to report to the authorities Forcing the abused to break the law

And the list went on and on. I'm surprised with all that I read. Until that point, my definition of abuse meant someone hit you. Like my dad.

Acknowledging I was in an abusive relationship was the first step. It was also the hardest. Maybe it was hard because things were not always that way. It would just appear sometimes, out of nowhere.

It was like the children's poem I remembered:

There once was a girl who had a little curl
right in the middle of her forehead.
When she was good, she was very very good,
but when she was bad, she was horrid.

Another session

Today we continued talking about abuse. I learn how people from dysfunctional families don't get to express their feelings. I learn that sometimes I deaden my feelings.

"Feelings are not right or wrong; they just are," Lauren, the counselor tells me. I never felt I had a right to my feelings.

I see I've repeated a pattern. As a child, I was afraid of expressing my feelings. Now in my marriage, I was feeling the same way. Unless I'm here in counseling.

At counseling, I feel validated. I can say or feel whatever I want. Usually, anger silenced me. The angry person trumps everyone else. But I'm seeing things clearer now.

If Mike is willing to get help, we'll be able to work on our issues. But if he's unwilling, what then?

"You need to have a plan in place," Lauren says.

But my mind has trailed off to another time. A time that broke my heart.

Anger is scary

It's 1980, Nathan is two months old. Mike is in the kitchen making breakfast, when suddenly he yells at the eggs he's making. Apparently some of the shell made its way into the pan. This is not the Mike I know. His anger is over the top.

I'm scared. And in a few moments, I make a decision. First chance I get, I'm taking the baby and leaving.

When Mike leaves for his college class. I call my friend to come and pick me up. Later, I call Mike, letting him know we're okay.

Each time I talk to him I feel torn. I know I'm keeping him from his son and it's ripping me up inside. And yet, I just want Mike back. The Mike I know, not angry Mike.

Within those two months I'm gone, he promises he'll get help. And he makes good on his promises. He would do anything to get his family home.

And now, years later, I'm being asked to consider separating? I don't know if I can do this again. My stomach hurts.

Have a plan

"You need to talk with your husband," Lauren said. "But before you do, find someone who will watch your children. Your talk should be without any interruption. Explain to Mike what you want him to do. And tell him what the consequences will be, if he chooses otherwise."

I feel a rock forming in my stomach. I'm a peace keeper. And she is asking me to stir up still waters.

I know she's right. But I also know how hard this will be. Mike loves me and the kids. But love is not enough. Safety has to come first.

Showtime

I drop the kids off at my friend Alice's house across the street. It's time to talk with Mike. He's reading a magazine when I walk into the living room. I sit down so we're across from each other. Eye to eye.

I remember being taught position is important in communication. Standing over someone comes across like you're an authority. It's better to be on the same level. My tone is calm, but my heart is beating out of my chest.

"Mike, I want to talk to you," I said, waiting for him to look up.

We need to talk, is never a good beginning.

"Mike, I've been thinking about it and I want you to get some help."

"Here we go again," he snarls.

Saying something positive will open the door. I need to share something I appreciate about him.

"Mike, I know how much you love the kids and how you want them to feel safe. But when you yell, they don't feel safe. That's why they run into our room at night."

"I never complain about that." he interjects.

"Yes, that's true. But I also know you don't want them to be afraid. You've gone to counseling in the past, but it's obvious you need some help again. You know I care about you, Mike. I've been doing some research and I've found a place that sounds like it might be good."

I pause and continue. "But, if you're *not* willing to get help, I'm going to have to take the kids and leave you."

There, I said it. But it feels like I thrust a knife into him. I can see the anger rise in his face.

"Fine!" he shouts. "Leave! I don't need you or anybody else."

I inhale. Now comes the hard part—the followthrough.

Oh, why do I have to do this?

I slowly lift myself from the chair, reaching down to get my purse. I have to get my kids and to retrieve the suitcase I dropped off at Alice's house yesterday. To take them and leave Mike. *God, please help me.*

I move towards the door. After about three steps, Mike yells out,

"Stop! Don't leave. I'll do anything you want."

And then, I exhale.

6. The Journey Continues

I'm so fortunate Mike's willing to get help. That's not the case with many women. As I mentioned already, we had embarked on the journey of counseling before. Each time we got a little further.

We learned to acknowledge problems, instead of pretending they didn't exist, and to face difficult things instead of hoping they would magically disappear—which by the way, never happens. There would be many bumps in the road, but we were determined to keep going.

The Minerth-Meier Clinic sounded like the right place for Mike. There would be extensive testing. There would be individual counseling and group counseling. They would cover all the bases.

It was a five week program but we had found a way to make it work. We would stay with friends while Mike was at his sessions each day. Then we would reconnect at night.

Blood tests show a problem.with anger impulse control.

Medication is prescribed. They explain it's like Mike has little seizures in his brain. He's given a medication like those who have epilepsy.

One day I receive a call.

"Your husband did not show up for his session."

I start getting nervous.

"I don't understand," I tell the counselor. "He left here this morning on time."

But the mystery is solved. The medication prescribed had made Mike sleepy. So he pulled off the road for a nap.

The doctor explains it will take a while to adjust to the medication. I sigh, hanging onto hope that in time, he will be okay. That we will all be okay.

Different opinions

We had listened to professionals before and followed their suggestions. One doctor's theory was that Mike's adrenal glands were shot. Going through stress, our adrenalin will pump; Mike's didn't. Consequently, stressful days were our worst days.

But how could we deal with that? Life had stressful times. Their suggestion was to give Mike some sort of supplements to help.

It's sugar

Years before, another physician diagnosed Mike as having hypoglycemia. Sugar became the enemy. So I adjusted his diet, removing all traces of sugar. Mike was also encouraged to eat small meals throughout the day.

During this time period, if Mike got angry I'd start questioning him,

"Have you eaten? You need to eat." Or, "Did you eat *sugar*? I bet you ate sugar, didn't you?"

Hope

And now these new tests he had show even different results. Medication will help with the imbalance in his system. As long as he takes his medication, no longer will he have outbursts.

I had lived with rage in my house as a little girl, and somehow rage found its way into my life again. And now this medication will keep rage under control.

Life became much easier for us.

But something strange is happening. Now that Mike's emotions were in control, mine seem to be all over the place. What is that about? Could it be I am finally free to express my feelings?

We tasted normal. Except for those times Mike forgot to take his medication. Then it was back to the roller-coaster-life we had known too well.

I became the medication police. And if he started getting irritable, I would ask him,

"Did you take your meds?"

I have to say, it is nice living without the outbursts. But if he gets irritable, I get nervous. Because in the past, irritability was the precursor to anger, and anger escalated to rage.

In the days before he took medication, Mike's anger would rise till he either yelled at the top of his voice, or he physically broke something. Then he would begin to calm down. I am thankful the medication frees Mike from those outbursts. He was so unhappy going through all the ups and downs. After an explosion, he would feel so guilty.

I remember learning about our brain and the emotions we feel in a psychology class. Our instructor talked about the part of our brain where our emotions lie.

"Class, once I was in a class and our instructor had a woman who had wires that were attached to her brain. As she sat there different wires were touched. And one moment she started yelling,

"Get me a phone directory. I want to rip it in half!"

I'm beginning to understand Mike in a new way.

He didn't choose to have these problems. All of us are wired differently. Sometimes we have faulty connections.

There were other factors at play. Things we were unaware of. Mike had recently begun a new job on third shift. While Mike's body tried to adjust to the changes, his mind didn't cooperate. His sleep disorder worsened, and the chemicals in his brain became off-balance.

Experiences in our lives leave imprints. And some of those experiences and how we react, stay with us for years. Sometimes for our whole lives. Mike had some traumatizing experiences. One that took place when he was just nineteen years old.

In the Garage

"Some black guy's in our car," Mike's brother, David, told him.

Following David outside, Mike saw their wooden garage door flapping open and shut. He didn't realize the storm he was about to see.

Inside their car sat their dad. He wasn't moving at all. After a heated argument with Mike's mom, his dad had walked out. Everyone thought he had left. But everyone was wrong.

Mike stared through the car window at his dad. The one who had bought him his first guitar. The one who would come and watch him play music.

Mike stayed there, waiting for the police to arrive. And he would spend the rest of his life trying to get that image out of his mind—an image still clear, though it happened so long ago.

Sometimes a dad can make a decision and his son will follow suit. Mike's dad attempted suicide and succeeded. Mike had attempted suicide as well. Would the pattern continue?

Like father, like son?

"Anne, is Nathan around?" Kyle asked on the phone.

Kyle was our son's youth pastor. A great guy, funny. But this wasn't a light call.

"What's up, Kyle?" I asked.

"I have reason to believe Nathan is going to hurt himself."

Nathan was fourteen at the time, a regular teenager, or so I thought. After that phone call, everything went in slow motion. I couldn't find my footing.

I'd like to say my mother's heart kicked in, that I was concerned about where he was and what was going on.

But, I must confess Instead I thought: *How could this happen and I not know? How could this be going on in my house and I not have a clue?*

We waited what seemed like forever.

Another call followed. This time it was my friend, JoHannah. Her daughter, Anna, had an idea where Nathan might be. They were on their way there.

Once again we waited.

Many stories that start out like this one don't end very well. We were fortunate. A lot of people were praying. Within two hours, Nathan was found. He *had* planned to hurt himself. Permanently. But when he went to the park to end his life, God gave him music.

Nathan made a short video and said, "I realized suicide was an option, but it wasn't *my* option."

Nathan uses his music to touch those who are hurting. He has a passion to help those who struggle with depression as he struggled. At retreats, when he shares his story, kids form a line, waiting to talk to him. Why? Because he understands the emptiness inside of them.

When difficult things happen in our lives, we can learn to work through them, getting through to the other side. And sometimes, we see a purpose to our pain.

But it takes all your energy to work through issues.

Some people feel the answer is to just forget your past, let it go. But after a while, the past you held onto now holds onto you. Tentacles wrap around tightly, squeezing the very life out of you. And pretty soon, all you feel is pain.

7. Make the Pain Stop

Trained professionals have helped my husband and me sort through so many hurts. Counselors have provided valuable tools to help us navigate through our wounded lives.

I sat in her beautifully decorated office. It was our first meeting, and already I knew I would be comfortable here.

Celia, a counselor suggested by Larry Crabb, looked at me with her caring, brown eyes.

"What do you want Anne?" she asked.

"I want the pain to stop," I said, my eyes filling with tears. "Make it stop."

Celia responded, "Anne, God never promised he'd make our pain stop. What he promised was, he would be with us in our pain."

I knew God would be with me. But at that moment, it didn't seem like enough. I wanted to stop hurting.

Week after week, I'd see Celia. I used up so many tissues and would come home thoroughly exhausted. But I learned things I never knew before.

It was Celia who first introduced me to the book *Boundaries,* by John Townsend and Henry Cloud. This was a new world to me. A world that seemed foreign.

And yet, people in that world were not merely existing, they were living. I started to understand about boundaries. The more I understood, the more I saw my need for them. So I could have my own space. Like a yard.

Boundaries

I need to ask you to leave my yard,
I know you've been here before.
It was I who would see you coming,
and throw open wide the door.
But you trampled all my flowers.
The advice you'd freely give
has drowned my little garden,
and the plants are few that live.
So I'm asking you to leave my yard.
I regret that my plea is so late.
I must get you to see that my yard is for me.
If you like, we can talk by the gate.
I also learned about marriage.

When Mike and I started having trouble in our marriage,

there were times I blamed myself. Maybe if I had made dinner sooner, or kept the kids quiet, then Mike wouldn't have gotten angry. But, it wasn't me. I just got good at accepting blame.

Marriage is work

You can put 100% into a marriage, from the time your feet hit the floor in the morning, till you fall exhausted in bed. But one person cannot hold a marriage together. It takes two. And if one is working against the marriage, it's only a matter of time before it dissolves.

From the time we were children, reading fairy tales, we were given an unrealistic view of life. The women between the pages were all carried off by their heroes. But fairy tales are not true, and it's disappointing when you realize your prince is not coming.

You can love someone, give them everything you have. But you're losing a fighting battle if they don't love themselves. Because, try as you may, you cannot make another person happy. It's really up to the person.

Some people have deep wells inside them. You can give and give, thinking you're filling his/her tank, but instead, you hear the echo as it reaches the bottom.

For some people, nothing will ever be enough. I've learned if we don't work on our issues, then unhealthy patterns will not be broken and may be repeated.

Wounded

I've learned we choose others based on how emotionally healthy *we* are. This explained so much to me. Peggy and I picked wounded men because we were wounded. Our choosers were broken. The way to make sure you have a healthy relationship is to *be* healthy.

Some of my coping mechanisms were not necessarily bad; they just didn't work anymore. Most of my life was spent trying to survive.

So eventually we get to the place where we realize we need new tools. Tools that healthy people use.

Celia saw me for quite a while. Then she thought group therapy might be good for me. I was familiar with group therapy. I would never forget the first group I had been part of, years before.

The Car Wash

"Today we're going to do an exercise," Sue, our group therapist, told us.

I could feel tension in the room. Her exercises hurt.

She told the eight of us, "I want you to get in two lines facing each other. All of you except Jim. This is called 'Car Wash.' Jim will walk between the two lines slowly. As Jim approaches, all of you can make circular motions with your hands, pretending to be giant brushes."

I lifted my hands to place them on Jim's back. It felt strange touching this person I didn't know. I wanted to recoil, to find a reason to be dismissed from the assignment.

I could hardly wait till it was over. And then, it was my turn to go through the car wash.

From the time hands touched my back, I cringed inside. But from the outside, you'd never know how I felt. I was a pro at hiding how I felt inside.

After our exercise, we sat down to discuss our feelings. "Which was harder for you?" Sue asked, "touching or being touched?"

While I found it awkward touching someone else, for me, being touched was excruciating. We all hated that exercise, but we learned so much from it.

Another time I became aware of my problem with touch was at a dinner with friends. As a friendly gesture, our host placed his hand on my arm to lead me into the next room. Tears slid down my face. I realized I had a problem with touch.

Baby Monkeys

Learning about my hunger for good touch was eye-opening. In a psychology class years ago, we learned about an experiment with baby monkeys.

Scientists separated the monkeys in two groups. In the first group, all the monkeys were cared for in every way. In the second group, (the control group), they received the same care with one exception: those monkeys were not touched.

The scientists anticipated the control group monkeys would develop at a slower rate than the first group. But what happened was the baby monkeys in the control group died. Touch is crucial to healthy development.

One of our first boundaries is our skin. Our skin keeps the good in and the bad out. But sometimes, this boundary is violated.

Potato peels

I'm twelve years old. Dad tells me, "Anne, peel these potatoes."

I tense up, knowing I'm not good at peeling. Standing over a garbage container, I peel away from me, just like I was taught. Suddenly, my face is on fire. My dad had slapped me hard.

"Don't waste the potato!" my father yells. "Look at all the potato you wasted.

I feel humiliated. Like I am worth less than the skins in the garbage can beside me. I want to disappear.

Abuse

Every time that I was hit,
it left a bruise inside.
And ever since, I've spent my life
just trying hard to hide.

Hitting a child arrests their development. I've often thought of what I'd say if I were to talk to the part of me that was abused.

"Anne, I'm sorry you were hit. No one deserves to be slapped. You did nothing wrong. I saw you trying your best —peeling takes a lot of practice. You have nothing to be ashamed of. You are worth more than potatoes—much, much more."

And then I'd wrap my arms around her, so she would feel safe.

Silence is not golden

Abuse isn't always loud. Sometimes you don't hear it at all.

"Mom, can I go bowling?" I asked.

I'm fourteen, and though I'm asking about Saturday, a work day, I'm hoping she'll let me go. Maybe.

"No. You know it's a work day, you have to clean the house," she said, without a thought.

But I'm having trouble letting this go. I want to feel like the other kids, to have some fun.

I know the rule. If mom or dad says "no," that's it. But at that moment, I don't care. I took a hammer and smashed that rule to bits.

"Dad, can I go bowling on Saturday with my friends?"

And dad said, "Yes."

And here I am bowling. I'm laughing; I'm having a good time, for the most part. It's just that my guilt keeps rising up. Why can't I just have some fun?

And now back home, I'm standing at the back door. It's time to go in and I'm scared. I slip in and see mom, but she pretends she doesn't see me. At least I think she's pretending.

I watch her talk to everyone else, acting as if I'm not here. It feels bad. One day turns into two. And here I am on the third day. She hasn't spoken a word to me in three days!

I cried. I pleaded. Nothing. I quietly put this lesson in my memory bank, very carefully making sure it doesn't get wrinkled.

Lesson to self: "You are not allowed to have fun."

At least that's the way I saw it.

I swear to myself I will never ignore anyone like she ignored me. And yet, I break that promise. More than once.

Codependent, me?

I learn a word I had never heard before; *codependent*. It means one person's happiness is dependent on another.

I used to be codependent. I didn't think I could be happy if Mike wasn't happy. It was a hard lesson to learn. The unhappier he was, the harder I tried to make him happy. Until I learned, you *can't* make another person happy, no matter how hard you try. I tried to make my mom happy too. That didn't work either.

I learned that codependent people display it in different ways: perfectionism, being a caretaker, being a fixer, being a rescuer.
Okay, it's a wash. I am *definitely* a codependent person. I have at one time or another displayed all of those things.

I remember feeling warm when someone would tell me, "I can't talk to *anyone* like I can talk to you." I felt important hearing those words.

I was somebody. In order for me to feel good about myself, I needed to be needed.

Otherwise, I didn't feel like I was worth much.

Learning to say "No"

Celia explained, if you love someone, you can accept when they tell you, "no."

"No" was not a word we used in my house when I was a child; we weren't asked things, we were told.

My parents laid down the law and we followed it. End of story. So I grew up thinking if people loved me, they would do what I wanted. They would always say "yes" to me.

If they wanted me to be happy, why would they tell me "no?" I learned that giving someone the freedom to tell you "no," means you trust them. Even when you *don't* understand.

I learned that I was demanding because I had a problem when people didn't want to do what I wanted them to do.

Me, demanding? No way. Now my parents were demanding, but not me. I asked nicely.

A light went on for me. I realized if I had an attitude when someone told me "no," it was because I wasn't requesting something—I was demanding. Ouch.

When I'm honest about my feelings, I don't have to become resentful. Resentment happens when we just stuff our feelings in. Nothing good comes from stuffing.

Saying what you mean

People from dysfunctional homes avoid saying what they mean. They say "yes" when they really mean "no." I learned when I do that, I'm not being honest. Ouch again. People can't read our minds; we need to say what we mean.

Did you ever hear someone ask, "What would you like to eat?"

And he/she responds, "It doesn't matter." And later you see that same person ticked off because it really *did* matter.

Enmeshment

With healthy boundaries, we see ourselves as separate individuals. People who have their own ideas, their own likes and dislikes. Without healthy boundaries, the lines are blurred.

Separate

I took a little piece of chalk
and outlined all my skin,
to understand more fully
where you end, and I begin.

Enmeshed people feel like they don't even exist. For so long they've just melted into the background.

Step Closer

Would you step a little closer,
just to let me see,
my own reflection in your eyes;
to see there IS a me?

People from dysfunctional families are so used to catering to the needs of others that they disappear altogether, leaving no traces behind.

The chair

I had anger. But you wouldn't know it looking at me. I remember the day our group therapist wanted us to confront people in our lives we had anger towards.

She carried a chair over and placed it directly across from me.

"Anne, who would you say you're most angry with, your mom or your dad?"

My parents controlled me. It became easier to just give in to them. I never had a voice. Inside, I was resentful with a lot of unexpressed anger.

I didn't want to do the exercise, so I lied.

"I'm not sure who I'm most angry with."

The truth is, I was afraid to stand up to either of my parents. I hoped if I told her I didn't know which one I was angriest with that she would go on to someone else. I was wrong.

Instead, she brought over a second chair,

"Okay, I'd like you to talk to both your parents."

I stared at the chairs before me, saying nothing. This whole thing was dumb and I was not going to say a word. But that didn't stop my therapist. After a few moments she said,

"Well, *I* have some things I want to say to them."

Standing before my two chairs she began, "Mr. and Mrs. Gollias, I want to tell you something..."

She told my parents how she felt. She told them they were wrong to treat me the way I was treated.

She got louder and was actually yelling.

My eyes opened wide. Her words sounded like she had been in our house, seen how I was treated. Like one day in particular.

Dad was hitting my brother George with a metal mop handle. Again and again, he struck him, despite George's pleas for him to stop.

I ran in the room and screamed, "If you hit him again, I'm calling the police!"

I don't know who was more surprised, my dad, George, or me.

But it worked, he actually stopped. He muttered something to George and left the room. I stood there shaking. That was the last time I heard those screams. The last time ever.

My therapist continued yelling at my parents, and then I said, "Now *I* have some things I want to say."

And there I stood, for the first time in my life, telling my parents how I felt. I started out quietly, and as I got in touch with my feelings, I got louder and louder.

Soon I was yelling at the top of my voice. A voice I hadn't heard before.

My Voice

Something happened and I found my voice;
it was a little crackly
and at first louder than it needed to be,
but I heard me.
I stood up for myself. I said, "No more."
I'm taking back what someone stole.

Working through my feelings would be a process. It would take a long time. But I had taken the first step.

In their book, *Your Parents And You,* authors Robert McGee, Pat Springle, and Jim Craddock talk about the role of our parents:

"They have the awesome responsibility of shaping the perceptions we learn by observation and experience. We apply these perceptions to our view of God, our self-concept, and our relationships with other people. The problem is that our parents are imperfect people who model beliefs and behaviors learned from their imperfect parents. As a result, our perceptions are often faulty, and we and our relationships suffer."

After a while I saw my parents differently. They were people. People who made mistakes. And just because they did things a certain way, didn't mean I had to follow suit. I could break some of the unhealthy patterns.

And that's what I chose to do.

Mind readers

I told my counselor, "It's funny. I realized, when someone is giving me a ride, I get surprised if they ask me for directions. Somehow I assume they know where I live because I'm with them."

He asked, "When you grew up, all your decisions were made for you, is that correct? And there were no secrets you kept from them, is that right?

I nodded. And then he explained,

"Well, because you had to share everything with your parents, they knew everything. And when you're with others, you assume the same thing is true about them."

What a revelation.

8. The Way We Think

It was a brain. The instructor opened a large jar before us and took out a human brain. Holding it in his gloved hands he asked, "Who would like to hold this?"

Was he kidding? My hand shot up, like a first-grader hoping to be chosen as line leader. I couldn't get the gloves on fast enough. Slowly, I felt the grooves in the brain. I marveled at how intricate it was. I couldn't believe I was holding a brain!

Doing things habitually creates ruts in our brains. Each repetition reinforces those pathways. The more we repeat our thoughts, the more the pathways are cemented.

I learned about those pathways in counseling as well.

Black or White Thinking

Sometimes people's thoughts harden like concrete, needing to be blasted now and again.

My parents were authoritarian, extremely strict. There was only their way, no other—and no questions. Growing up in a dysfunctional home, there *is* no in-between. Things are simply good or bad. Black or white.

Black or White

There were no shades of color
in my world of black or white.
There were no grades of justice,
but simply wrong or right.
And holding pieces of my life,
like puzzles—meant to fit,
I tried so hard to force them in,
until at last, I quit.

With black or white thinking, people use words like always and never.

I had to be right

I love garage sales. My friend, Lois, and I walked up the driveway. And then I spotted it: Rummikub, a game I enjoyed years earlier. And the tag said one dollar. Yes, I love garage sales.

The smiling woman who took my dollar said, "You're going to like this game, it's with letters."

"I've played this game before," I smiled back. "It's with numbers."

Her eyes sparkled as she handed me my game. I hardly took a step or two when Lois said,

"You just *had* to say that, didn't you?"

"What?" I responded.

"You just HAD to correct her."

"She was *wrong*," I argued. "I had that game."

And then Lois responded with words I would always remember,

"What *difference* did it make?"

For years, I thought it was my job to set things right. Correcting others, convincing them I knew what I was talking about. Being right mattered more than people.

Once was not enough

Sometimes I need lessons repeated. While taking a biology class, I met another returning student. Our quizzes had just been returned.

Barb struggled accepting that one of her answers was wrong. No matter what the teacher's assistant said, Barb refuted it. Then Barb shut down completely.

My husband's words echoed in my mind,

"Anne, sometimes when I'm talking to you, it's like a metal door slams shut and nothing can get in."

Now I understood. I had to see it in someone else. Now, I wanted to change. I didn't want to be like that.

I couldn't shift

In one counseling session, my counselor listened as I spoke,

"Sometimes, I get in a frame of mind, and even if I want to move, I feel stuck. Inflexible."

Romita said, "I believe your shifter is broken."

Listening to her, it resonated with me. That was exactly how I felt. If I could just get my shifter fixed, I knew it would make my life easier. And not only mine, but my family's life as well.

She gave me a valuable tool that day. A question to ask myself when I feel stuck. The question is, *"What if I'm wrong?"*

Though simplistic, it was enough to open myself up to the possibility I could be mistaken. I felt my cemented thoughts start to loosen. I felt the metal door start to life.

Little steps can make a big difference.

Another day, Romita showed me a picture I had seen once before in a psychology class. It was the image of a young maiden with a feather in her hat. Inside the first picture sat another picture, an elderly woman with many wrinkles.

"When we're stuck," Romita explained, "It's like we can only see one of the pictures. People who get stuck in their thinking have trouble believing they could be wrong."

I shifted in my chair, reflecting on the years I had spent convinced I was right. Bound and determined to let others know. I could almost feel the chains start loosening.

I Should...

Another day, while in a session with Romita, she made an observation.

"Anne, you seem to have a lot of rules in your life."

And I couldn't disagree even if I wanted to. She was right.

Rules

I live my life by many rules
all written down in stone,
And I feel so exhausted,
and often, so alone.

The rules I've made keep driving me,
and though I've kept so few,
These rules are not for me alone,
there's also some for you.

I'm the one who incorporated these rules. I lived with so many restrictions growing up. And though my parents have been gone for years, I still operate as if the rules are in place. This is a difficult pattern to discard. I'm still in process.

My rules have been a measuring tool, something to give me a sense I was managing things. Except I wasn't.

Mike noticed it years ago when he told me, "I wish you could see yourself, Anne. You follow the kids around, ordering them, 'Pick that up. Put that away.' I never see you relax. And you never let them just play."

He was right. I didn't know how to relax. I only knew how to work. And I resented those who could relax.

When things got out of place, I tensed up. Sirens went off in my mind. Someone was going to be in trouble.

And trouble always meant being hit. So I'd spend countless hours making rules to make sure everyone operated accordingly.

Perfectionism

I learned about perfectionism, which was really hitting home with me. When people come from dysfunctional families, so much of their life is out of their control. So they find areas they can control, and keep at it until they are perfect, or close to it.

I opened the linen closet door, tightening up inside. How many times had I shown Jessie how to put our towels away? How hard could it be? You just fold them a certain way and make sure you line them up.

A perfectionist is a type of controller. The perfectionist gets bent out of shape if things aren't done the way he/she wants them done.

As a recovering perfectionist, I still see traces of living that way. Now when I see things that are done differently than I'd like, I either change them myself, or I try shifting.

People are worth more than towels.

Years ago, I'd make sure every hair was in place before I left my house. In addition, I'd check to see if my smile was on. No one knew me. Not really.

Inside Out

Don't be fooled when you look at me;
things are not as they seem to be.
The smile I put on carefully,
does not reflect the inner me.
It cannot hide the pain inside.
So don't be fooled when you look at me.

People Pleasing

A dysfunctional family generally caters to one member. It doesn't take long for the remaining members to feel their needs are unimportant.

After a number of years, the identities of others in the family disintegrate.

Promises to Keep

Exhausted from her crowded day,
she lies across her bed,
taking two more aspirin
to soothe her pounding head.
Mentally she ponders things
and all she has to do,
grumbling that her work's undone,
although it's nothing new.

*Covered with resentment,
at last, she falls asleep.
Tomorrow there's so much to do,
and promises to keep.*

People pleasers eventually become resentful, realizing their own needs are not being met while they meet the needs of others.

After all you've done, doesn't anyone care about you? When will it be your turn?

Being a caretaker consumes any time for dream-making. Caretakers adhere to the schedules of others, living their lives accordingly.

Sometimes a caretaker makes the mistake of doing things for others which they are capable of doing themselves. This fosters an unhealthy dependence on the caretaker. And the person they take care of becomes irresponsible.

In their book, *Boundaries*, authors Townsend and Cloud tell the story about a couple who see a counselor concerning their adult son.

"He doesn't do anything," they complain. The counselor listens and then asks, "Where is your son?"

"Oh, he wouldn't come," they explain, embarrassed. "He said he doesn't have any problems."

"He's right," the counselor responds. They gasp in unison.

"What do you mean?"

"Well, you make his decisions, you clean up his messes, you take responsibility for him. He's right. He doesn't have any problems. You do."

It *is* good to help others. But sometimes we do too much for them, and by enabling them, we end up hurting them.

Caretakers are giving, selfless people. A caretaker's identity sometimes gets wrapped up in what he/she can do. But our worth is not determined by what we do. We have worth because of *who we are.*

The more I received counseling, the more I grew as a person. As I worked on issues, I started seeing myself as separate. My husband's problems were his, not mine.

I've Grown

I see us as two people
—separate, not enmeshed.
I'm only responsible for me.
I used to carry him;
it got to be too heavy
I can hardly carry me at times.

His dreams hurled him out of bed again;
I heard him moan as he crawled back in.
It's hard watching someone tormented,
trapped inside their own nightmares.
I love him. He didn't choose this.
I wish his life had been different;
I wish he didn't hurt so much.
I'm sure he wishes that, too,
but for now, at least he's sleeping.

Layers upon layers

I'd work through some of my emotions only to discover more underneath. My problems were layered. I had to learn to stop stuffing things away in my emotional closet. Stuffing emotions doesn't work, eventually they all fall out.

Hiding

Buried deep within us
are secrets we have kept;
regrets for things that we have done,
or times we felt inept.
Piling layers over hurts
we tried so hard to hide.
And no one really sees us now;
we're hiding here inside.

It was liberating to come out of hiding. To acknowledge my feelings instead of denying them. Pain would rush to get out of my closet as soon as the door opened.

Pain

Again my pain woke me while turning,
and reeling and feeling a yearning for peace.
I searched and I strained for an end to my pain.
But instead, all my tears were released.

I just kept finding more and more layers of pain.

Droplets

Droplets drizzle down the pane,
all mingled with my tears again,
and I cannot see clearly
through my rain.

Peace eludes me, hope excludes me,
isolation reigns;
and I no longer try to stop my pain.

I learned that all the years I spent avoiding pain, I had actually prolonged it. I used to hear people say, "Time heals all wounds."

It's not true. Time alone does NOT heal us. In order for healing to begin, we need to acknowledge our pain and embrace it. Then God can work.

Beneath my pain was a layer of anger. I resented my hurts. Maybe because I never had the right to express my feelings before. I'd stuff my feelings down, but they'd still find a way out. Sometimes they'd leak out.

Angry Tears

I wasn't one to fight at all,
I never did it well.
And when I did get angry,
I couldn't even yell.

My anger lived inside me
all locked away for years.
The only way I let it out
was through my many tears.

Sometimes my anger frightened me. Maybe because when I used to see my dad angry, pain followed close behind. Someone got hurt. And even when I started learning how to express my anger, I wasn't certain I did it right. It was all new to me.

Where Can I Put my anger?

I pull back, shooting the innocent with my bent bows.
They run for cover.
My mouth is pursed, my eyes narrow,
I grind my teeth—where can I put my anger?

Emptying out my emotional closet, I recognize it's a job that needs to be done periodically. Resentments pile up quickly.

An anger workshop

I'm sitting in a workshop about anger. The speaker just listed different kinds of anger. I'm waiting till she gets to Mike's anger. My arms lay on the table before me, but they may as well be folded across my chest.

Go ahead, try and teach me, my arrogance whispers. I know all there is to know about anger.

And finally, she talks about explosive anger. The kind I've witnessed too many times in my life. The kind that causes me to quiver. Whether we're talking about my dad and his waving belt, or Mike who'd erupt without warning.

Would she like me to come up and give examples?
Focus, I tell myself.

And then the speaker describes another anger, a silent one. I shift from side to side, glad Mike isn't here. I listen, or at least try to.

Did she really say what I just heard? That being silent when you're angry is one of the most dangerous kinds of anger there is? Suddenly I feel less uppity.

It takes time

We live in an instant society. Drive-throughs enable us to get meals within moments. Counseling is *not* instant. It takes a lot of work and a great deal of effort.

After a while, you begin to recognize signs that indicate you need additional help. You aren't processing things well. You're becoming overly emotional without apparent reason. Maybe it's time for a checkup.

Panic

I think about the days my panic would win. I'd be fine, when suddenly I'd start getting anxious.

Running to the fridge, I'd start throwing containers in the trash. Cartons with a little food left in them. Until the fridge looked like I felt—*empty.*

Empty

I'm sitting in a church office. We are in need of help. The person in charge of the benevolent fund sits before me.

"I need you to please fill out this form so we know how we can best help you."

Later at home, I look over the paperwork noticing all the blank spaces. And then it hits me, It's as if I'm…

Hardly Here

I'm missing who I used to be
when I would be with you.
It's like I lost a part of me
I was accustomed to.

Somewhere along the line, having lost so many loved ones, I felt abandoned. And I wondered, do I have the right to live when they are no longer here? The term is *survivor guilt.*

When someone you love dies, you feel like part of you has died too.

Before I know it, I'm back in counseling. As Mike and I struggled, the stress level rose like mercury on a thermometer, and I couldn't stop crying.

My life story is almost memorized from the countless times I've shared it. I notice I'm using fewer tissues for each session. That's something.

I'm writing down my feelings this time and bringing those papers with me. Many of them take the form of poetry. It's how I think.

I share with Dr. Phillips the stories that become this book. And while I'm sad, I notice that is not the only thing that brought me here. My other emotions are desperate to be heard. It's time to deal with them.

As long as I'm alive, I'll be dealing with issues. Some over and over again. But now as they surface, I no longer push them down, ignoring them. Instead, I face them and embrace them.

Permission to enjoy life

In his book, *Making Peace With your Past,* Tim Sledge mentions that people from dysfunctional families struggle with positive things in their lives. He talks about having a fear of joy. He's talking about me.

It makes perfect sense. Any time I started to enjoy anything, I wait for the axe to fall. Wait for something to stop the joy.

And even today I struggle with this.

In February of 2013, my book, *Real Love: Guaranteed to Last*, was launched. I was excited, and believe me, that is an understatement.

Another axe?

On February 18, my brother George was having a procedure done. A stent was being put in his heart. I could feel my anxiety stirring.

Just two years earlier, we said goodbye to our brother Gus. Pancreatic cancer came and robbed him of his health. It was painful. I remember when he leaned forward one day and told us,

"I'm so glad I won't have to go through this with one of you guys."

With George in the hospital, I became nervous. I didn't think I could go through something like that again. I knew I didn't want to.

Steve

By Thursday, my anxiety level had risen. I felt a pressure in my chest.

"Mike, I think you should take me to the ER."

And in moments we were there. The nurse explained what would be happening as soon as I entered that room. It was just as she said. People came at me from all directions. There was no room for modesty as strangers began attaching wires to my chest.

I was told my blood pressure was off the charts. My stomach hurt, so a nurse came in with a drink for me.

"This will eventually numb your mouth, but it will also take care of your stomach ache," he said.

I had to tell him, "You look like my brother Steve." Brown eyes, like all of us in my family, and dark hair. Yes, he looked like a younger version of Steve.

I asked Mike, "Don't you think he looks like Steve?"

Mike mumbled, "A little."

When the doctor left the room, Mike followed him. I was to stay overnight in the hospital. They were waiting for test results.

I said goodbye to Mike and was wheeled upstairs. Maybe I could get some rest. God knew I'd need it.

In the morning, I met my roommate and a room full of her family members. It wasn't long before Mike arrived with Jessica to take me home.

After I introduced him to my roommate, Mike rose to his feet, all tensed up.

Immediately he blurted out words that still shake me to the core:

"Something terrible happened. Your brother Steve had a heart attack and died."

I heard myself screaming, "No! No!"

Instantly my husband and daughter were by my side. The curtain was pulled to give us a false sense of privacy. No, Steve couldn't be dead; I just talked to him a few days ago. Steve was fifty-two. No.

But I couldn't deny it. It was my terrible reality. So two days later, we traveled to Chicago. We stood at the gravesite full of other family members. And once again, I said goodbye to a loved one.

At the funeral, I met his friends who said, "Oh, *you're* the one who wrote the book."

And the trip that was to be a celebratory trip turned into a different kind of trip altogether. Perhaps God wanted to protect me when I got the news. To make sure my blood pressure was monitored. I don't know.

Steve had died the night I saw the man who looked like him. When my husband asked the doctor if he could tell me, he was advised to wait.

Once again, I felt like enjoyment was pulled out of my hands. That happiness was for other people, but not for me.

It became easier to prepare myself for something negative. That way if it happened, I wouldn't be so disappointed. And if I fell, I wouldn't fall far.

The problem with this thinking is, that it's faulty. And it will prevent me from engaging in something I might enjoy. Even buying myself something small.

I have trouble spending money on myself, even if I'm given a gift card. Recognizing this was painful. It reminded me of someone else, mom.

The cocktail dress

Mom opened the box. I remembered how pretty the dress was—a shimmering gold and mint green.

Dad smiled when mom tried it on for him. Then her words cut through the air,

"When would I wear something like this? All I ever do is work at the restaurant."

She threatened to send back the dress. Mom didn't make empty threats. The dress left one day. Another delivery arrived the following week. We watched her open the box, taking out two fresh uniforms in plastic bags.

There was no smile on her face. She quietly walked out of the room to put them away.

I'm sad my mom was so sad. But it was a choice she made, I'm not her.

In his book, *Healing is a Choice*, Stephen Arterburn, says, "The power to heal physically, emotionally, and spiritually is in God's hands. But the choice to be healed is yours….Maybe you wonder when God is going to take the hurt away."

I'm reading this book because I want to keep healing. We don't get to a place and say, "I have arrived." We can keep growing and healing as long as we are breathing.

For years, I wondered why I had so much pain. I wondered why others seemed carefree. Wanting to work on my issues is hard. But it's a choice we can make. No one can make that choice for us.

9. What does Healthy *look* like?

Barbara Streisand used to sing the words, "People who need people are the luckiest people in the world."

We were created to need others. Significant people with whom we can share our lives. Unfortunately, when we come from troubled homes, we find relationships that are less than healthy.

If it was never explained to you, and the only relationship you saw modeled was your parents' relationship, how can you even recognize abuse? The relationships we witness become our templates.

And the images we saw flickering on our television screens or magnified on theatre screens were skewed. We saw what others reflected to us. All that information was gathered in our developing brains. We were incapable of deciphering what was good without an accurate model. It wasn't possible.

You will be drawn to people who are at the same level of health you are. So, if you want a healthy relationship, you need to make sure you're healthy.

Unhealthy relationships	Healthy relationships
one person is in charge	there is give and take
one person makes decisions	both voices are heard
there is fighting	there is discussion
there is suspicion	there is trust
there is isolation	each has other friends
dependence on each other	there is independence
growth is discouraged	growth is encouraged
there is no privacy	there is privacy
one hurts another	there is kindness
one puts down another	there is mutual respect
one is over the other	the two are side by side
there are lies	honest communication

Which list do you resonate with? When someone speaks to you, is it from a place of mutuality? Do you feel like a child being reprimanded?

Are there clear boundaries in your relationships? Are those boundaries respected?

If you feel people walk all over you, or you feel used, the problem is a lack of boundaries, or your boundaries are being ignored.

Do you have the freedom to share anything on your mind? Do you feel shame? Do you feel put down? Do you walk on eggshells? Are you constantly worried how others will receive what you say?

People *do* need people, but we need people who will respect us. Everyone deserves to be respected. But first, we have to respect ourselves.

Regarding relationships

I asked people as I was writing this book, what questions they had about domestic violence or abuse.

One question was: What things should you look for in another person?

When I asked Dr. Jim Phillips what things are important in getting to know someone, here are his suggestions:

Emotions can't be trusted

When you're in the beginning stages of a relationship, don't let your emotions dictate things. Physical attractions are great, but they should not be determining factors.

Take your time

Never formulate your opinions too quickly. People can show you a version of themselves in the first three months, which mysteriously disappears.

Look for discrepancies

Discrepancies are sure to surface. Some people are better at hiding their negative traits from others. Remember in the beginning of a relationship, people have a tendency to show you their best side.

Look at the friends he/she has

Does this person have a lot of friends? How do their friends treat him/her?

Communication is essential

Does the conversation keep going back to him/her as if magnetically pulled? Is there a lot of the pronoun, "I?" Does your opinion matter at all?

Parental respect

If you hear this person talk about his/her parents, do you hear positive or negative things?

Is there a lot of complaining?

If a person is self-centered at the onset, this will get worse as the relationship continues. If what you are seeing is not good, don't believe things will get better. Why would they?

Respect is vital

Generally speaking, people will treat you the way you let them.

In their book, *Boundary Power*, authors, Mike S. O'Neil & Charles E. Newbold state that people are mistreated because they lack boundaries in their lives. People without boundaries are not respected. It's much easier to look outwardly and blame those who mistreat us. But the responsibility lies with us.

When I first understood this concept, it angered me. I didn't want to accept responsibility for how others treated me. It was easier to blame them.

Telling people what you will and will not tolerate is a way of taking care of yourself. When you've gone through life neglecting yourself, you feel disregarded. It will feel like others are mean.

People who grew up in abusive homes learn to silence their needs. Why verbalize a need that will never be met?

It's a method of self-protection. They just don't want to be hurt again.

If I don't set my expectations too high, I won't be so disappointed. The problem is, this doesn't work. I know, I've tried.

Get on your own list

All of us have lists in our lives. Things we need to do, people we attend to. People from dysfunctional homes have many lists. But sadly, their names won't be on anyone's list. They *hope* someone will attend to them, they *wish* someone would, but it doesn't happen.

A healthy person acknowledges his/her needs. It's okay to need others, it's how we were made. And though others may let us down, closing ourselves off from relationships makes us feel isolated and lonely.

Pastor Jim Powell shared in a sermon, "Though people need others, sometimes those with the biggest needs withdraw from others. Then they blame people for not figuring out what they need."

The people around you

A healthy person becomes aware of his/her relationships.

I remember one exercise in group therapy where we were made aware of the influence of other people around us.

Our therapist passed out large pieces of white paper.

"Today we're going to look at the people in your life and determine what kind of influence they've been. Put your name in the very center of the paper and draw a circle around it. Then write down the names of people you know with this in mind.

If they are relatively close to you, place their names close to yours. Try not to exclude anyone you interact with. Include people from work, school, church—from anywhere.

After you're finished writing down their names, go back and insert either a (+) or a (-) sign by each person's name, based on what their influence is the majority of time. If it's *both* positive and negative, put both signs there."

Looking over my paper, I felt sad seeing so few positive influences. Could that be why I felt so lonely? In becoming a caretaker for others, I had neglected myself. And I resented the fact no one seemed to care about me.

Negative people drain us. They are like withdrawals from the bank. We need positive people who'll make deposits in our lives.

Looking around the room, I realized the value of the people around me. We were all there because we wanted to become healthier.

We were told, "You may have to withdraw from some negative people in your life."

I cringed hearing that. I didn't know how I would do that. It's like I somehow felt obligated to stay in relationships that were unhealthy. To receive from others both good and bad. And sometimes, it was mainly bad.

She continued, "You may choose to keep some of the negative people in your life, maybe they are family members. What you can do in that situation is restrict the amount of time you spend with them."

Even that was news to me. I would subject myself to long periods of time with those who hurt me. As if they mattered, but I didn't.

Get help

When life became too big for me to handle I acknowledged I needed help. Initially, this was hard for me to do since I had become so self-sufficient. Refusing to rely on others made me lonely. My resentment kept me company.

And trying to protect myself from disappointment, it got easier and easier to disconnect from life.

We live in a society which encourages independence. Some people see getting help as a sign of weakness, while the opposite is true.

It takes courage to admit you need help. That you're not effectively processing things in your life.

Be courageous. Admit you need help instead of pretending everything's fine. Invest in you.

Get to Work

Going to counseling is hard work. When I first started seeing a counselor, I came home exhausted, sometimes needing a nap. You can't unlock and deal with feelings

stored away for years without expending a great amount of energy.

Each session I spent with a counselor, I received valuable tools for navigating my life. Some I never knew existed. The survival tactics I had learned in my family of origin were ineffective. They made things harder.

Counseling *is* work. Accountability reminds you that you are not in this alone.

Counselors are trained to help us children who are trapped in adult bodies. They understand we have areas where we need to grow. They recognize we haven't been

nurtured. Patiently, they will help us learn how to grow ourselves up.

Pastors join the list of potential helpers for hurting people who need clarity to move forward. Life coaches are also valuable in assisting when things become difficult.

Never let the lack of money stop you from getting the help you need. There has never been a time I needed counseling that God did not provide the resources.

If you're attending school, there are counselors on staff willing to help you. Most agencies have sliding scales, which provide discounted prices.

Group therapy is less expensive than individual therapy. Lastly, some churches provide counseling. They call them lay counselors.

Imagine a life where you are productive, realizing your purpose. Imagine getting up every day with energy for the things you want to accomplish, instead of feeling depleted and resentful. Imagine finally living your life instead of merely existing.

You *can* live life with people who support and encourage you. You can have people around who believe in you. You don't have to imagine that life. It can be yours.

Fired

As I listened to good counsel. I began getting some ideas of my own. One day while trying to process my anger towards my parents, I became aware of something.
Even though they have been gone for years, I lived as if they were still in my life. No longer did I want to feel as if I were under their power. Like I was working for them.

I walked in my counseling session with papers in my hand and a grin on my face. I decided to take the power back from my parents.

My paperwork stated that I had been employed by Stanley and Mary Gollias, as of such and such date. It further stated I would no longer be working for them. But instead of a type of resignation, I decided to fire them.

My letter was professional, including a place for the signature of a witness.

"Would you be willing to sign this as my witness?" I asked my counselor, hoping he'd realize I was serious.

"Absolutely," he said.

Signing my paper, he validated my decision. It was done. Official and complete.

Firing my parents helped me feel empowered. It has not been immediate. Little by little, I am taking my life back. Learning how to grow myself up. It would not be instant, but neither were all the things I had gone through.

My real father

Another time, I imagined how different my life would have been without the parents I had. What if there had been other names on my birth certificate instead of theirs?

Copying my birth certificate, I took a bottle of white-out from my desk. Carefully, I covered their names on my copy. Aware of my sadness, I kept going. In my mind, it had to be done.

With their names gone, I then wrote in another name where it asked for the name of my parents.
Just three letters, but it said it all: God.

After my mom and dad were gone, I remembered

reading the verse in Psalms 27:10. "When your father and your mother forsake you, I will take you up."

Oh, how I needed that reminder. God had parented me longer than anyone. So I gave him that spot. I'm not going to lie. It was hard to do this, but in a way, I was acknowledging something important. My parents are gone. I needed to accept it once and for all. I had a life to resume, one that was waiting for me.

10. To the Hurting

There's a chance you're reading this book because you know someone in an abusive relationship. Or maybe *you* are that someone, and you're wondering what to do. My heart goes out to you.

Maybe you've picked up this book hoping to find some answers, some direction. Maybe you need hope.

If you want to get out of an abusive relationship, here are some practical suggestions:

Tell someone about your situation.

Don't try to do this alone. It doesn't get better on its own. You need support—help from friends, family, clergy. People you trust. Don't wait too long. Enlist help now.

Have a plan.

When things become chaotic, our thinking gets muddled. You need to have a well-thought-out plan. This includes a safe place to go. If you need help with your kids while you talk to your significant other, ask someone.

There are people willing to help. Today there are agencies available in many places. There are shelters for the sole purpose of making sure you and your children are safe. Make yourself aware of everything out there.

Be persistent

This situation requires perseverance. Even writing those lines, I feel sad—sad that anyone has to go through this, sad for your feelings of helplessness. You didn't think it would be like this. No one deserves to be abused. It's your responsibility to make sure you and your children are safe.

People who abuse others have a problem. Some may get help. Others blame those around them, not willing or able to see the problem. They believe the problem lies outside of themselves.

I wish I could talk to you face to face. I want to stress that you are a person of worth. You have value. I want you to know you matter. When a person hears negative things long enough, they start to believe them.

I Tried

I tried to believe the nice things you said.
I actually held them in my hands for a while,
but I was muscled out of them
by shame and disgust.
They've been with me a very long time
and think they're family.

One question answered

I'm sitting in the waiting room of the auto department at Sears. On the television is a story about domestic violence. There are only two of us in this room: me and another woman.

"That's really sad," I said, looking at the television.

When the woman nods her head, I share the story about Peggy with her. I look for any opportunity to share my sister's story. I want God to use it to help others, wherever they are. Even in an auto department.

I share with her, "There were times I felt tormented, thinking about how my sister died. Being bombarded by all sorts of images. And in my darkest moment, I remember hearing God whisper to me, 'Anne, I was with her.' That made all the difference to me. When my sister took her last breath, I believe God picked her up and carried her to heaven."

The woman responded, "I've been the victim of domestic violence too."

I listen as she tells me her painful story. Finally I say, "May I ask you a question?"

"Sure," she responds.

"Why didn't you tell your family what was going on sooner?"

This question was locked up inside me. A question I needed to have an answer to. It's not about this woman at all; I'm still trying to understand things.

She responds, "Well, there were really two reasons: I was afraid he might hurt my family, and I was ashamed."

In that moment, this person I had never seen before gave me a gift. She looked at me and said, "I'm sure that's why your sister didn't tell you sooner."

I felt the tears slide down my face. Tears that would bring more healing.

Shame

I've just finished a book titled, *I Thought it was Just Me,* by Brené Brown, Ph.D. Dr. Brown believes we can develop a resiliency to shame. She explains that part of the reason we feel shame in our lives is because we believe we're the only ones going through our struggles.

We also feel shame because we keep things secret. Dr. Brown believes the way to get rid of our shame is to expose our secrets and surround ourselves with people who are empathetic.

The difference between feeling guilty and feeling shame is when you feel guilty, you feel you have a problem. With shame, you believe you *are* the problem.

The special tea

I'm sitting here with my mom, excited. It's one of the first things we're doing that heralds my upcoming graduation from grammar school. I feel important sitting here dressed up. It's just Mom and me, and those times are special because there are so few.

Mom is enjoying herself when one of my classmates takes the podium. This is the silly part. They are going to announce what we bequeath to the seventh grade class. I'm excited to hear, but a little nervous too. They start mentioning things, but not everyone is laughing. And then they get to my name,

"Anne Gollias will leave her long fingernails."

Immediately I close my hands to hide my short nails. I feel warmth in my face. I try to keep tears from coming, but I'm not doing well. I can't even look at Mom. I just want to disappear.

Oh, why did I have to be a person who bit my nails?

I somehow get through the rest of the names, hoping the next part will be okay.

As they begin announcing what we are most likely to become in our careers, I feel myself tense up. I haven't recovered from the first put-down yet.

And then I hear, "Anne Gollias will most likely become a director of a Blind Date Club."

I feel everyone's eyes on me. It feels like the whole world is laughing at me. Once more, I can't look up. I'm not even sure what they meant, but it doesn't feel good.

While my classmates always talked about going with this guy or that guy, I wasn't allowed to be part of it. But I never realized it made me a target. I sat there feeling so odd. I had tried hard to blend in with everyone, but this was proof I never made it.

This day that was supposed to be special has turned into something else. I have a knot in my stomach that may never untie. I just want to get out of here.

I shared this story with my counselor who told me, "The fault lies with whoever was in charge of the event."
But, as that seventh grader, those words pierced my young heart, and I felt shame.

When we share our shame, we quickly realize we are not the only ones who are suffering. We discover we are not the only ones with problems. And in acknowledging this, our shame diminishes. This is why support groups are so valuable. The groups help us dispel shame, so it doesn't cling to us.

A Magnet

*I seem to have a magnet
that's deep inside my head,
and I repel what's positive
and keep what's bad instead.*

Compliments are hard to receive when you're used to hearing put-downs. We like compliments. We just think they're meant for others, not us. On the other hand, the negative we believe immediately.

Compliments

*Compliments are hard to hold,
they're just so slippery.
But any criticism said
—just sticks so readily.*

After time, the negative things you tell yourself will not affect you the same. You'll learn how to replace them with positive things.

At first, you'll argue with yourself. Expect it. Fight it.

One thing you can do is write affirmations—positive statements about you or about life. Write them out every day. Here are some examples:

I deserve to be safe.
I am a person of dignity. I have value.

I wrote my affirmations every day. As much as ten times each. I was intentionally refocusing my brain from the negatives I've heard, often from myself.

The only way to refute lies is with the truth. And when we believe the truth, lies don't affect us the same.

You are a person of value. Not because of what you look like. Not because of what you do. Just because you are.

God knows you completely. You're important to him. The same God who knows when one sparrow falls.

A Sparrow

I saw the smallest sparrow
that I have ever seen.
It wasn't perched upon a branch
but kind of in between.
And as I watched this little one
I never saw before,
God whispered, "I love sparrows,
but I love you even more."
I needed that reminder,

I needed strength anew;
I needed God to lift me up
as only he could do.
So now whenever I go out,
I hope that I will see
reminders of my Father God,
and of his love for me.

I don't know where you are in a relationship with God. Sometimes when we've had a lot of pain in our lives, we're angry. But instead of sharing our anger with God, it becomes a wall between us.

Sometimes we hold things against God. And yet, God knows it. This is what God once told me regarding the things I held.

Open Your Hand

What is that you are holding in your hand,
in your fist that is closed ever tight?
What is that you are purposely
keeping from me,
for you feel you have the right?
Don't you know as you grow
in your walk with me,
I can see even things that you hide?
Oh, if you only knew
what's in store for you,
you would open your hand so wide.

When I pushed my anger down inside of me, thinking God wouldn't know, I was wrong. He's the one who created my feelings.

But I want you to see an accurate picture. When I got help, it was hard. I didn't sail through. It's still hard. And I still get help.

Even though I forgave my dad on his deathbed, I still had anger inside. There were more layers I needed to work through.

And when I released anger at those two empty chairs in group therapy, was that the end of my anger towards my parents? The short answer is *no*. I realized I had more work to do. Work that would be hard, but work that still needed to be done.

Empowered

I need a belt. I remember seeing belts in a thrift store, so I make my way over there. Two dollars is fine; I'm not particular. This isn't a gift, although in a way it is. A gift to myself.

Yes, it would have been nice if I had Dad's belt for this, but I can pretend it's his belt. I got good at making stories out of reality and dismissing my reality as a bad story.

Holding the belt, images parade in front of me—bad ones. I finger the belt, remembering the pain. I wipe fresh tears away as I remember younger tears.

For years I had asked, "*Why?*"

I remember as a child, reading that Jesus was beaten. I sensed he knew how I felt. He knew about the pain and humiliation. With scissors in hand, I cut the leather. Each cut brings me pain. Like the pain I felt hearing my siblings cry. The pain I felt when I pleaded with him to stop, and he wouldn't.

Gus got it the worst. I shook, hearing Dad yelling words no one should ever hear—hateful words.

When Gus was about eight years old, he shared with Mom, "Don't you *get* it? He doesn't love me."

No eight year old should ever feel that way. Snip by snip, I cut the belt out of my life.

I don't know how many hours I've been here. My hands are sore from cutting. I'm using kitchen shears to do the job. How fitting. Dad worked in a kitchen. I was slapped in a kitchen. This is the most important job these shears will ever have.

My throbbing hands tell me it's time to quit. For today. I am learning how to embrace my pain instead of avoiding it. My stomach hurts.

I let myself feel the anger, the pain. I take in a deep breath and look at the pieces before me. The power is leaving.

With me

*I'd touch the places on my skin
you hit repeatedly,
and started to believe that there
was something wrong with me.
But if I could erase one day,
I think that it would be
the day that you slipped off your belt
and started hitting me.*

It's day two. I pick up my baggie full of belt pieces and go at it again. It has to be done. No one will know this was a belt when I'm through with it. Just shredded leather.

I feel a stretching inside. Like somehow my hurt little girl inside me is becoming freed. No longer do I need to keep telling her, "It's okay. You're not alone." Instead, I have entered this pain with her. And I'm here to stay.

The next day I go to the counselor's office. I walk in with my baggie in my hands.

"What's that you have there?" He asks.

This wasn't an assignment. This was just something I knew I had to do.

He tells me, "The only thing that identifies this as a belt is the metal buckle."

He hands me back my little bag as my tears slide down my face.

I sit and hold the very belt that held me for years.

Grief

I had other issues to work through: dealing with everyone abandoning me. I'd look around and notice other families. Families that seemed happy. It was like rubbing salt in my open wound.

I'm sure there were other families who had lost loved ones, but my pain kept me focussed on me, not them. Besides, feelings rarely care about what's true.

I can't hear someone else's pain while mine shouts.

Anger coats my sadness. I have a hardness forming around my heart. Anger I'll have to work through. God was on my list.

How Dare You, God

I stood before an empty sky
and shook my fist clenched tight.
I opened up my very soul,
and screamed with all my might,
"How dare you, God!
How dare you,
take everything of mine,
while people all around me

seem happy most the time."
I've watched you take my loved ones
from in my family.
And I can't take it anymore,
so get away from me.

With silence all around me,
I wait for him to leave,
like others who have disappeared
when I would start to grieve.

I feel his arms encircle me,
and hear him gently say,
"I know that you're upset with me,
but I am here to stay.

There I was pushing God out, just like our father told us after he hit us, "Get away from me."

It has taken time, but eventually I am learning God can handle our anger. He really can. But first, I needed to give myself permission to work through this anger. I used to just clam up, hoping it would go away.

Working on my anger

In the past, when I didn't get my way, I felt unheard. Sometimes I'd shut down. My anger would start me, but it was my stubbornness that kept me there.

At those times, my husband tried to get me to talk, but he wasn't getting in. No one would.

"Look at those clouds," he'd say. I'd look up at the sky. I'd try. I knew what he was trying to do. Part of me appreciated his efforts—a small part of me that *wanted* to talk—but still, I kept silent.

Locked

I'm locked within this mind of mine,
and cannot find the key,
Until I see the prison guard
and realize it's me.

One day, when I was in this angry state, I forced myself to talk. I felt myself fighting it. *Just keep quiet. They don't care. No one cares.* I ignored what I told myself. I made myself talk.

I could hear a chain breaking. It was a heavy one.

Now when I'm angry, I use words. The temptation to clamp shut is there, but I try not to give in. And if I'm not ready to let the words out of my mouth, I at least say, "I'm angry now, but I want to talk about this later."

Another emotion we experience is sadness that no one knows how we feel. After all, we've had so much happen in our lives. We feel sorry for ourselves.

Pity

*Today I wear pity
like a comfortable sweater
with sleeves that don't fit.*

*It's better than nothing
against the cold apathy of others;
at least I'm covered.*

*Sure, I'd like to be wrapped in warmth
as I imagine love.
But love is elusive and out of reach.*

*So I settle down
in my favorite chair
with my sweater on and no one there.*

When I was a little girl I don't remember soft touch from my mom—unless I had a temperature. Then she'd gently touch my forehead. As a young child, I confused fevers with headaches.

I would run to her saying, "Mom, I think I have a headache; feel me."

Grief

I used to believe, if I don't think about the loved ones I've lost, it means I didn't really love them much.

I heard a story about a man who lost his son in a fire. When the father recovered his son's bones, he carefully put them in a box. He carried that box with him everywhere he went. That box of bones defined him.

Some thirty years later, there was a knock at his door. Standing there was a young man, "I am your son."

The older man listened as this young man explained how he had been taken years ago, and how a fire had been set to cover up the kidnapping. The father listened to every word. Then he closed the door on his son.

His son's death was his reality. To him it was bigger than life. Perhaps I've also been carrying a box of bones.

Box of Bones

*My arms are weary carrying
this box of bones around.*

*And yet, somehow I know I cannot put it down.
You see, it has defined me to everyone I see.*

*And if I'm seen without this box,
no one will know it's me.*

I wish the effects of abuse could be smoothed out like newly formed wrinkles in fabric, but they can't.

Still on the journey

We're at my brother George's house. Yesterday was a bad day. My husband and brother got into it. It was a first. Ugly words were said. Today's got to be better.

Please God, can today be better?

But our days are made up of choices, choices people make. Before we made this long trip, my husband tried to tell me he didn't think he could do the three and a half hours. I wish I would have listened.

My plans became more important than my husband. Some decisions have grave consequences.

Almost a Widow

I'm sitting with myself by myself again.
I was almost a widow tonight.

I heard him shake his pill bottle.
I knew he was in a dark place;
I pretended to sleep,
something I learned a long time ago.
His speech was slurred;
his movements were slowed.
I saw the note on the floor,
reading it without surprise.

He almost left me again.
I feel empty and alone, waiting

—this is hard.
I know it's hard for him,
but watching feels harder.
This is time number four.
How can I get on with my life
waiting for his death?
He's really already left.
I'm sitting with myself by myself again.

Not again

I'm angry. I've finally learned to express my emotions and I seem to be stuck on anger. Actually, I'm way past anger.

How could he even think of suicide? Are we worth nothing to him? He has a family: two grandsons who adore him, a daughter and a son. And what about me?

I don't want to go through this again. And yet, it stares me in the face. What do I do? I'm trying hard to understand. Is he okay now? Will he try again?

Our ride home is quiet. I look back and see him sitting there. I know he's in there, imprisoned. I thought we were past this.

Every day took effort—effort I no longer had. Nor did I have strength. The truth is, God helped me stand. And then he helped me walk.

I can't think way into the future. I don't have grace for that. But I have grace for today. And God will provide what I need for tomorrow. He always has. And he always will. How do I know? God doesn't change.

From the Inside

I love him,
but the love is mixed with sympathy.
I wish his life had been different.

I wish he didn't hurt so much,
but I can't help him with his hurts
— I'm filled with my own.

He's loved, but he doesn't feel it, ever.
I can't fix him; I know I've tried.
He's the kind of broken
that can only be fixed from the inside.

I'm going to have to forgive him. It won't be the first time. And the thing about forgiveness is, it won't be the last time either.

God will help me forgive him. Just like he always has.

Forgiveness

I'm at the homeless shelter. It's my job which started as

an eight-week internship. I've been here about a year now.

I lead a grief group and a second one about boundaries. I tell them,

"Today I have an exercise I want you to do. As I pass out these pieces of paper, I want you to think about someone who has hurt you—someone you have not forgiven.

I tell them to write down the following:

I cannot forgive you for _____.
To forgive you would mean _____.

Pencils move around me. I see someone crying. I give them about twenty minutes for this exercise.

"Would anyone like to read their answers?" I ask. I listen as one guest shares her pain. It gets quiet again.

Another person answers. There is a bite in his words. I'm proud of his courage in sharing. He must feel safe here.

"What should we do with these papers?" I'm asked at the end of our session.

"You have a few choices," I tell them. "You may take them with you. You may throw them out. Or you can leave them with me. If you choose to leave them with me, just know that I'll pray for you."

I just came across the papers tucked in my desk at home. Everyone turned them in. What courage I saw that day. Forgiveness takes courage.

Your Past

In *Making Peace With Your Past,* Tim Sledge talks about forgiveness. Forgiveness is where a lot of people get stuck.

Sledge says, "In order to forgive someone we need to understand what forgiveness is *not.*

- *It is NOT forgetting.*
- *It does not mean the other person was right.*
- *It does not mean the pain vanishes instantly.*
- *It does not mean the other person controls you.*

Forgiveness is something I'll have to do over and over again. And when I think I have a handle on it, another memory surfaces, forcing the door of my emotional closet open.

Healing takes time

Healing will take time. But time will pass regardless of what we do. We may as well work on our issues.

In order for change to happen, we must first acknowledge something is wrong.

I love the quote by John Pierpont Morgan: "The first step to getting somewhere is to decide you're not going to stay where you are."

When you heal, you are not only freeing yourself from negative emotions that bind you, you're also freeing yourself to feel positive things in life.

You can't have one without the other. Yes, you will hurt like you've never hurt before. That's true. But there are positive emotions you'll also experience—emotions that have been dulled or buried deep within you. It's time to let them out.

It's so worth all the work it takes.

When you feel joy, and trust me you *will* feel joy again, it will be like technicolor compared to black and white.

Trust the Process

Dr. Jim Phillips explained to me, "We make the mistake of thinking life is linear. It's not. It's cyclical. Healing is a process. There will be steps forward and other days we'll find ourselves struggling with issues again. Think of it as a spiral that keeps circling and still moves forward as it goes around. There will be days you'll feel you're not going anywhere. But you are. You need to trust the process."

I hate the spiral, but I see it clearly. It's a continual movement, even on days I felt I was not moving at all. I was growing.

Maybe I'm *not* where I want to be yet, but I'm not where I was before.

I Had fun

I became one of them for a couple of days.
You know who I mean, don't you?
Someone who does things, goes places.
It was nice.
I saw my reflection in a store window
and can testify it was me.
But part of me was still disconnected.
I had fun—partly.

I would be introduced to the concept of being happy. Something I hadn't felt in a long time.

I Tasted Happy this week

I let myself smile and didn't wipe it off.
It was the real kind of smile,
not the kind you put on
when someone is around.

I wanted to wear it longer,
to actually keep it for myself,
but guilt convinced me
I should be satisfied
with little grins and half-smiles

—it's all I deserve.
With head down I agreed
and handed back my smile—I miss it.

We need to remind ourselves that we never arrive. If we start thinking we're done, we're setting ourselves up for disappointment.

There are days when I'll do fine and then other days my emotions take me on a ride. A ride I don't feel like taking.

My ride

This week I ran all over the place,
letting my emotions run my train.
My sadness brought me low through valleys.

My anger brought me through forests with thistles,
and thorns that scratched at my sore arms.

Guilt made me want to sit alone,
stewing in things I had said or done.

Shame made me get off the train for a while,
convinced I didn't deserve to ride.

*I did have a patch where I looked out the
window and saw the same sun that shined on others.*

*My face warmed with rays of light.
I smiled for a long time,
but other voices became louder and familiar.*

*It's not that I haven't tried to silence them,
it's just that they are stubborn,
knowing just the right buttons to press
to get me down to size.*

*And then I sit and ride the train
where I don't want to go,
strapped in by my own insecurities,
unable to move,
just along for the ride—again.*

Stuck Again

*Disillusionment strangles my hope.
Things are not as I thought they were.
Negative thoughts flood my mind.*

*People fall off pedestals, on top of each other.
The fog lifts once more.
I stand knee-deep in disappointment.*

My feet are immovable—stuck in:

Why bother? I told you so.
What were you thinking?
— all in my own voice.

I scrape visible traces of gum off my shoes.
My movement is slowed.

Everything seems to be working.
I'm having trouble restarting
— I've lost my zeal.
The next thing is not THE thing.
I have to take one step
—just one.

There are days I'll feel misunderstood. Other days I'll feel alone. And the world around me doesn't seem open to how I feel, but instead, how they would like me to be— fine.

Just Fine

I'm so mad I can't see straight.
Once again, I'm left—in a heap, discarded.
I didn't know my expiration date was up.
I never know that, not even sure when it is.

But it must have been.
It's the same feeling each time,
the packaging just slightly changes.
I guess there's just so much of me people can take.

*And then they back up,
disappear—sometimes permanently.*

*I'm angry, but you can't tell.
The tears throw people.
It's never been safe to be angry.
People tell me I have the right to be mad.
But when I show them one angry look,
when I raise my voice, they stop.
They can't handle it.
So I get back in place,
saying the words they want to hear,
wearing the face they want to see.*

*I'm ticked, but don't know what to do with it.
So quietly, I fold it back up and put it away
with all the other uncomfortable feelings
I don't have a right to.*

*Oh, you asked me how I was?
I'm fine, just fine.*

If you're hurting, you need to know, you're not alone. I've collected some stories of others who are in pain. Others who are hurting just like you.

11. Other Stories

Stories of abuse are everywhere. And they do not only happen to women. Some stories of abused men are hidden. Abused men feel emasculated. They get laughed at—are considered weak.

I attempted to get stories from men for this book. Though I spoke to a few, they were not ready to put into words the pain they experienced. Personally, I know men who are hurting as badly as women who were abused.

I know someone who got divorced years ago. The reason? Abuse. Her husband would get drunk and go after her.

No matter how many times I hear about domestic violence, there is a part of me that refuses to believe it goes on. I know it does, I hear the stories, but to me it's awful and I don't want to believe it.

Pain is universal. The following stories are true. Only the names have been changed.

Sara's Story

It was in the 1970's when I heard a story that made me cringe. Sara and Greg had been married for a few years. Sara was a nurse, and she and her husband had a two-year-old son, Danny. Sara's marriage was failing and she decided she would seek a divorce.

As in many cases, that's when things heated up. Exploded is more accurate. But even so, no one expected what happened next.

One day Greg went over to his father-in-law's house to see Sara. Within minutes, he pushed his wheelchair-bound father-in-law out of his way, making his way over to his wife.

Taking out a gun, Greg shot his wife, their two-year old son, and himself. In a matter of a couple of minutes, a whole family was wiped out. Greg had often threatened Sara: "If I can't have you, nobody will."

Those of us who knew them were shocked. We tried to comfort Sara's sister, but how do you recover when someone is tragically pulled from your life?

Those that remain are left with the debris. They have to find a way to cope and try to continue on.

Jean's Story

It takes tremendous courage to involve the police in domestic violence. I couldn't call the police—I was mortified because I *was* the police.

I could compartmentalize my professional life and was successful at work, but when I got home, I was emotionally crippled by guilt. My husband was a violent alcoholic from a long line of alcoholics. As with most abusers, he started with emotional abuse, which escalated quickly to physical and sexual violence.

He convinced me that I was a failure and everything was my fault. Because we had met at a Bible study and he professed to be a Christian, he sometimes literally beat me over the head with scripture. It took me years to seek counseling help from a great Christian man who, over the course of two years, helped me extricate myself from the marriage.

Prior to that, well-meaning people gave all kinds of horrible advice. One tidbit is burned into my memory: After my husband attempted to kill me, a Christian advised me to stay in the marriage because, "He hasn't killed you yet, has he?"

After six years of torture and years of counseling, I secretly rented an apartment. I had hired movers to transport my few belongings before my husband came home from work.

A year later, I went through with the divorce.

Unfortunately, that was not the end of his reign of terror. He swore he would kill me, and that I'd never see it coming.

Until the day he died, I drove with one eye on the rear view mirror.

I have to admit, I did the dance of joy when I heard he was dead. I firmly believe God doesn't waste anything. Not our pain, our tears, or our experiences. Although I would never want to experience domestic violence again, it gave me a hard-won credibility in my professional life.

Domestic abuse became my *forte* on the street. It takes a victim to truly understand a victim.

My experiences with alcoholism gave me the heart to teach a drug and alcohol prevention program to thousands of children. In spite of all the good that came from my pain, I still wear the scars, and struggle with questions that will only be answered in heaven. I don't think a person truly recovers from domestic violence. At best, it's an ongoing recovering process.

Angie's Story

My name is Angie, and I have been in a domestic violence marriage. My ex-husband was abusive mentally, verbally, emotionally, and physically. He first abused me when we were engaged to be married.

He fractured my wrist, and I remember my friend telling me I should leave him and not marry him. My exact words were, "He didn't mean to do it, and he'll change when we're married." Sad to say, that didn't happen—it only got worse.

He was very controlling and jealous. What made the matter worse was that we were both drug addicts, so he was very physical under the influence of drugs. He smashed my head into a cement floor one night—all I could see were stars—and he hit me with a small baseball bat, breaking some of my top teeth.

He would always tell me how much of a piece of poop I was, how ugly and fat I was, that if I left him, I'd never find anyone because no one would want to be with someone crazy like me.

I used to always say I'd rather get physically hit because the cuts, bruises and broken bones would eventually heal. The emotional and verbal abuse took years to heal. I wanted to leave him so bad, but was so scared. He told me one time if I ever left him, he'd kill me, and I believed him.

Plus, I really believed what he told me about being fat and ugly, so I had no self-esteem.

It wasn't until we were on a drug binge, after I had my son and I got arrested, that I got away from him. I had to do some time in jail, and he was still off on the binge. He then went into treatment. That was my break.

I felt strong without him. I got some of my self-esteem back and didn't want my son to be raised in an abusive family. I finally told him that I didn't want him coming home after he was released from the treatment center.

A few months later, after eight years of marriage, I filed for divorce through the courts using a personal ad because he had taken off again on a drug binge.

Until you're in that circumstance, you can't tell someone what to do. I wish I would have told someone about my abuse and sought help much sooner. Back then, it wasn't like it is today with doctors or hospitals asking you if anyone is hurting you.

Seek help immediately, or leave the relationship at the first sign of any abuse. It does not get better, and things don't change. For the longest time, until I sought help, I thought if a man didn't treat me abusively, he didn't love me. Crazy, isn't it?

When my son was about three or four years old, I had problems with my son hitting me. I would tell him,

"It's not nice to hit me."

He would respond, "Daddy did."

Domestic violence affects the whole family. If you think your children are not affected by it, you're wrong.

Children are a lot smarter than you think. I sure didn't think my son was old enough to know what my husband was doing to me—yet he did. He thought, if mommy or daddy does it, it must be okay.

Lucy's Story

I sat next to my mother and tried to console her. She finally broke down fully and admitted, "I am afraid he is going to kill you."

It was impossible to respond honestly to my mother and relieve her fears at the same time. She knew I had been in a dysfunctional relationship for seven years and saw no way out.

She was not, however, even remotely aware of the severity of the situation. I had not divulged that he was not merely controlling. There were alcohol and drug addictions impacting the situation as well. Strangers would knock on our door in the middle of the night to buy/sell drugs.

Over twenty years later—and finally healthy—there are three things I wish others had known at the time:

It would have been better if someone had encouraged me to leave the mess. I only had one conversation with my mother and not one conversation with another person about the situation. Everyone knew but stayed silent.

In the middle of the mess, logical options don't always make sense to the person who is being abused. The abuser can manipulate the situation so strongly that up feels like down.

What the abused needs most is unconditional love. They will make the appropriate steps when they can. Distancing yourself from the abused only makes things worse.

Susan's Story

Domestic violence affects the whole family. Susan Murphy Milano witnessed her father, a decorated Chicago Violent Crimes Detective, brutally and violently attack her mother repeatedly.

The words "If you leave, I will kill you" turned into reality the night Susan walked into her childhood home and found her mother murdered and her father in the next room dead from a self-inflicted gunshot wound to the head.

But sometimes the events in our lives determine the path we will take. Since the murder-suicide, Susan made significant changes in the way the world looks at violence in and outside the home. This quest for justice was instrumental in the passage of the *Illinois Stalking Law and the Lautenberg Act.*

Susan Murphy Milano was a specialist and expert in intimate partner violence and worked nationally with corporations, faith-based organizations, domestic violence programs, law enforcement, and prosecutors to provide technical and consulting services in high-risk domestic violence and stalking related cases.

Her principal objective was to intervene before a victim was seriously injured or killed. Utilizing a procedure which she devised, the Evidentiary Abuse Affidavit, Murphy Milano's clients are all still alive—a statistic that is remarkable considering the distinct increase in intimate partner homicides.

With every breath she took, Susan was determined to help other women so they would not experience the loss she went through. Sadly, she lost her battle to cancer in October 2012.

Her books, *Defending Our Lives*, *Moving Out, Moving On*, *Time's Up!*, and corresponding strategies are taught worldwide and used by law enforcement, social workers, attorneys, health care workers, human resource departments, and domestic violence agencies. The comprehensive strategies and escape plans utilized by Susan have been successful and tested by time for over twenty years.

Susan's last book, *Holding My Hand Through Hell*, is a memoir of her personal story.

Chris's Story

My father's school breaks were always terrifying for my mom and me. He drank all day for weeks on end and abused us whenever he wasn't passed out somewhere. We cowered in fear, hoping not to upset him. It never worked.

He yelled for me again. "I'm coooming," I said. Ten o'clock in the morning, and he was clearly already drunk.

He yanked me down the last few stairs and to the ground. Standing over me he growled, "Son, I'm gettin' tired of you not listenin' to me. It's time to teach you a lesson you won't soon forget. I think it's time for the board —The Board...of Education.

He took me out to the backyard shed. He pointed to several two-by-fours and asked me to pick one. My father winked and grinned, then said, "It's for The Board of Education, son."

Shaking, I picked one. He smiled and hugged me. "Thatta boy! You got a good eye for wood—makes me proud."

He grabbed the two-by-four and dragged me over to the table, where he pulled out a Sharpie marker and drew the shape of a paddle on the wood. He handed me the board and pointed at the jig saw. Then he said, "It's time to cut The Board of Education, son!"

That's when I started crying. Uncontrollably.

Furious, he ripped the board from my hands and hit me in the back of the head. "I said it's time to CUT the BOARD, son!"

So slowly, I cut the board, flinching each time he moved, never sure what would happen next.

"Now it's time to let'er breathe."

He handed me a circle cutter and told me to cut six circles in the The Board of Education. I froze, just thinking about what my father would do to me with it. My hesitation cost me again.

Uppercut to the gut. He picked me up from the ground and placed the circle saw in my hands again.

"Let...her...breathe," he said.

So I cut the holes and then sanded the board down under my father's watchful eyes.

"Time to decorate." Using three colored Sharpies, I christened the two-by-four in red, blue, and green: THE BOARD OF EDUCATION. He held it up with a smile on his face. "You should be proud of your work here, son. Now let's see how well this baby works."

With that, he swept my legs and grabbed me by the waist. He threw me up against the table, legs dangling in the air. Ripping my shorts off, he paddled me. I don't remember how many times.

The creation of The Board of Education scarred me more than the beating. He never used The Board again. He didn't have to. He would just ask me, "Son, do I need to consult The Board?" I would immediately cow into submission.

My mom left my father not long after that.

Beyond The Board

Fast forward about a decade. I had become a Christian, but there was a deep distance between me and God. I started praying about this distance, and the Lord whispered I had bitterness toward my father.

"No, I don't!" I retorted with a bit too much passion. Maybe I did have some business to attend to, after all.

So I decided to spend Christmas with my father, strictly out of obedience to God, not any love for my father.

He picked me up at the New Orleans airport, and we had a three-hour drive to Vicksburg, Mississippi.

Awkward conversations started and stopped, the result of two strangers and years of anger.

"How was the flight?" he asked.

"The woman next to me talked my ear off."

Stilted laughter. A full minute of silence.

"How's work?"

"No complaints. Keeps me busy."

More silence.

Eventually, my father stammered out, "Chris, did you really come out here because God told you to?"

"There is no other reason I would want to see you again, Dad," I started. "The pain you caused, before and after the divorce, scarred me. But I refuse to let my relationship with you hinder my relationship with God."

I stared at him.

"Son, I just don't feel like I deserve God's forgiveness. Not after everything I've done. What do you have to say about that?"

"If you are planning to earn God's forgiveness, you're screwed. We all are. God's forgiveness is a gift. You don't earn a gift."

Then, for the next two hours, we continued talking about forgiveness. With tears streaming down his face, he pulled the car off to the side of the road.

"Chris, what do I do? I feel so lost."

A few minutes of silence passed in the car as I struggled whether to give my father a free ticket to heaven or let him stay condemned—as if I got to decide.

I didn't want him to be accepted by God. I wanted him to pay for his sins by going to Hell.

He deserved it.

But the longer we sat there, the more I realized I was no more worthy than he was, so I relented. I led my dad in a prayer to become a Christian on the side of the freeway between New Orleans and Vicksburg.

His life has never been the same. He stopped drinking that very night. He tells everyone that God sent his son to introduce him to Jesus, the Son of God. He is a regular member of a church. He is learning what it means to love his current wife.

I am not saying my dad is perfect. Far from it. He still has his narcissistic moments. He still lacks understanding of social expectations. And I'm not suggesting that people who commit abuse should not be held accountable for their actions.

What I am saying is that no one is beyond God's grace. Not even me, not even my dad.

When I look back on The Board of Education, I see no redemption. It seems God was absent, maybe busy—worrying about someone more important.

I wish I knew why He didn't intervene and keep me safe. But I am glad to say the story doesn't end with The Board of Education.

12. Conclusion

I feel this fight within me. I knew what he asked me to do, I just didn't want to do it.

Hadn't I opened myself up enough?

And yet, one thing is certain. I recognize resistance, having lived with it for so long. My fear of what others think is still alive and kicking inside of me.

This is like that one time I had a speaking engagement. Just like it. There I stood in front of a group of women. And I heard it clearly just as I was about to speak.

"I want you to tell them about the time you were bitter."

"You want me to tell them what?" I tried arguing.

But over the years, I had learned to listen to that voice.

And so I told them about my bitterness. About how I actually had gotten mad at God. I shared things that I have shared in this book. And what happened next?

Well, it surprised me when it didn't change my demeanor, not one little bit. Just then, I saw a woman approaching me. She looked directly at me and said,

"You were talking about me."

"What do you mean?" I asked.

"Everything you said about bitterness, you were talking about me."

At times I find that I still fall into bad patterns. I start caring about what others think, I make them bigger than they are. And the results do not satisfy.

Mike's medication was messed up a few months ago. It threw everything off, and I mean everything. Once again, the world spun around so fast it took all my energy to get through the day.

When I have a bad day it feels much like it does in the middle of winter. A winter like this. It feels like Spring will never come. A gray film covers everything. And I don't have the strength to lift it off. At the time, I don't see it as a temporary thing.

One good thing that emerged from that week or two is how far we have come—how much better things are today.

A Little More

And now it's March. I thought this book would have launched in February. That's what I planned. But things did not fall in place. I thought logistics were postponing things. A foreword that would be done, the cover.

I kept wondering why things weren't working out with the book, when someone I deeply respect asked me,

"Could it be there's something that's still not in your book?"

Come on, God. How much more do I have to share?

And then I remembered that speaking engagement where God told me to talk about my bitterness. He is the reader of hearts. He knows what people need to hear.

I still struggle. I have PTSD, Post Traumatic Stress Disorder. For those who may not be familiar with it, let me share what it's like.

You could be going along in your day when all of a sudden you feel thrust back in time. And the things you are experiencing no longer feel the same. Why? Because somehow you are no longer operating with an adult mind. Instead, your capabilities are limited. Like this time.

I saw the flashing lights in my rearview mirror. I hoped the police car had someone else in his scope, but my hope faded quickly. My heart started beating fast and here came the tears I tried holding back.

"Do you know how fast you were going?" the officer said. It was a simple question, but I didn't know the answer.

But he knew how fast I was going, and he proceeded to tell me. My mind went to our finances, and if I got a ticket, I didn't know how we were going to handle it. I felt like I was in trouble. And for me, that button is a very bad button.

Being in trouble signaled all the adrenalin my body could muster up. Being in trouble meant getting hit.

The tears came. I saw the officer was uncomfortable. He tried telling me it would be okay. He could have helped an adult, but in those few moments, I was a blubbering child.

I'd like to say I paid the ticket and that was the end of it, but it didn't happen that easily. I decided to go to court.

And on that day, I sat surrounded by other lawbreakers just like me in the courtroom. Where was the judge? Wasn't I to see a judge?

I watched carefully as a man in a suit called out names. Maybe I'd get a clue as to what I needed to do. Maybe the judge was in another room. But one by one, people just left.

Hearing my name called, I shot up like a bullet. I tried to listen to the words spoken by the man in the suit. Was he talking too quickly or had my ears started hearing slowly?

He said nothing about a judge. He just pointed me to a room to pay my fine. I took out my checkbook, wrote a check with the money earmarked for the utility bill, and remember asking about a driving class. The clerk barely looked up. She's disgusted with me, I thought.

When I got in my car, I burst into tears. But still it wasn't done. I was to attend a driving class a couple of weeks later at a community college, but never received information about which building it was in. But how hard could it be?

I arrived there and felt my heart beating fast. To my surprise, there were five buildings. I chose one. As I walked the empty halls, I remembered being tardy at my elementary school so many years ago. I could even hear my saddle shoes clicking on the floor.

I realized the empty building at the college was not the right one for my driving class. I went back to my car and met someone who kindly helped me locate the correct building. I ran in, spotting a woman behind the counter.

"I need room 101," I said, breathless.

"No," she said abruptly. "You're late, you may not go in there."

"Can't I just explain to the teacher?" I began.

No," she repeated. "But if you like, you can signup for another class, but you *will* have to pay again."

I mumbled something about signing up online and almost ran out of the building. Forty-five dollars gone, and I hadn't even taken the class. In my car, I dissolved in tears. I knew I needed to wait till I could drive home.

I felt worthless, stupid, just like dad told us we were.

It wasn't the police officer who started this whole episode, it was how I felt being around authority. When anyone becomes the authority in my life, whether real or imagined, a button gets pressed, and once again I am a child.

The problem is, I never know when the buttons will go off. I never know.

Faking it

I've come to a realization. I've done a lot of faking it. I had to in my family of origin. I wasn't free to be who I was.

"Stop that crying."

I learned to give people what they wanted. After all, they mattered and I didn't. The problem is, I ended up denying who I was because of fear. Fear has occupied too much of my life.

I struggle

The truth is I still struggle. And I probably always will. For some reason the picture of Bozo's circus pops in my mind. They always seemed to have a plate spinner on there. I try spinning plates too. Different parts of my life. I'm not very good at it.

Don't get me wrong, I can get a couple of them spinning pretty well, maybe even a few. But when it's more than that, in the corner of my eye I can see them wobbling. Slower and slower they move, until one of them crashes to the floor.

I look around and feel like everyone else is a professional plate spinner. Not only do their plates spin, they seem to do it with such ease. I used to be amazed, used to think one day that will be me. But I realize it's not going to happen. I've come to accept that I may only successfully spin a few plates, and that's okay.

Now what?

I love good endings, don't you? It's great when everything fits nicely in place. But I'm afraid that's not what my book does. It's not what life does either. Life is messy.

People have problems, and there *are* loose threads. But life is a process, we're still growing.

A Matter of words

In the course of writing this book, I've discovered some things about myself. I don't think like everyone else.

I remember telling Dr. Phillips, "I don't want to feel different, I just want to be normal."

He responded, "Normal is boring. I want you to replace some words you tell yourself. Instead of saying the word *different*, use the word *unique.*

Don't you want to be unique?"

"Yes," I smiled. "I'd like thinking of myself as *unique*."

"And instead of saying you just want to be *normal*," he continued, "replace the word, *normal* with the word *mediocre*. Do you really want to be *mediocre*?"

I could feel my mind changing as I thought about his suggestion.

"No. I *don't* want to be *mediocre*," I said.

What about you? Instead of trying to fit in and be like everyone else, maybe it's time we put our efforts into being the people God made us to be —individuals.

Missing pieces

You wouldn't believe the number of hours I spent on pagination the last couple of days. I couldn't understand why I didn't succeed. I even resorted to doing it manually.

Yes, I really did that. And when I got finished and scrolled through the pages before submitting the book, I found every number had changed! At one point they were all the same number!

I felt like I was in an episode of the old television show, *The Twilight Zone*.

In fact, in my pagination frenzy, I became a perfect illustration of what insanity is: doing the same thing over and over, expecting different results. My inner dialog was:

What's wrong with you?
Why can't you do this?
You just need to try harder.

I was certain it was me. *I* was the problem.

Today I took a deep breath regarding my pagination. I acknowledged I must be missing information.

And though I had suspected it earlier, this time I refused to proceed till I researched it more. So I googled it once again. I read more about the particular program I was using, I viewed tutorials. I did my homework.

Doing it faster, longer, or with more enthusiasm hadn't worked. Our lives are like that. We can try our best, but if we don't have all the pieces we need, we still won't be able to accomplish what we set out to do.

Sometimes we can give it our all, and it's still isn't enough. But the thing is *we* are enough. No matter what anyone has ever told you.

My hope

I hope as you've read my book that something has stirred within you. I hope in some way you've been encouraged. I also hope things in your life work out for you, I really do.

Life is hard. You'll go through things you never would have chosen for yourself. You'll have struggles and you'll hurt. And sometimes you'll feel like you're alone.

But the truth is, you're not alone. Not at all. You see, we're all broken.

Dear Reader,

I want to thank you for picking up my book. For taking a look into my world. I know this subject matter isn't easy. Some people would rather not even think about it. But there are others who have found themselves in it, wondering how they ever got there. Wondering if things will ever change.

For those of you who have never experienced abuse, but know someone who has, I think it's great that you care enough to want to understand it.

If this book has helped you at all, I'd love to hear from you. Writing this has been one of the hardest things I've ever done. But I don't want anyone going through abuse to feel hopeless. If you are in an abusive situation, please, tell someone. And please, don't wait like Peggy did.

I'm praying for anyone who reads this book. Praying you will one day feel free to live the life you were meant to live—a life that's safe—a life you fit in. And I'm praying you'll be free to be who you really are.

Please feel free to share this with others, it's giving my sister a voice again.

Warmly,

Anne

About the Author

Anne Peterson is a poet, speaker, and the author of 14 books available on Amazon.

Among her books are children's books, poetry books, and art books she has done in a collaboration with her daughter, Jessica.

She is also the author of forty-two published Bible Studies as well as a hundred articles with publications such as Christianity Today, Today's Christian Woman, Crosswalk, and Medium.

Anne's poetry is sold in gift stores throughout the U.S. as well as in twenty-three countries.

If Anne is not writing, she is probably spending time with her favorite little people: her grandchildren. And you can bet she's smiling big.

Follow Anne's writing:

www.annepeterson.com
www.facebook.com/annepetersonwrites
Medium: https://medium.com/@annegolliaspeterson/latest
Pinterest: https://www.pinterest.com/annepeterson2
Instagram: https://www.instagram.com/annepetersonpoet/

Made in the USA
Middletown, DE
12 May 2023